Sunday Is Not Enough:
Devotional Readings through the Week

By the same author

Chorando por Brasil: Crônicas de um Pastor Que Olhou Para Trás
(Portuguese Memoir)
This Week at Home: Devotional Readings between Sundays
(Lectionary Year B)

Sunday Is Not Enough:
Devotional Readings through the Week

Joel Mark Flugstad

Lawler Street Book Concern, LLC
Oklahoma City, Oklahoma

Lawler Street Book Concern, LLC
2015

Cover Photo: Bells at Christ Our Savior Lutheran Church, Chickasha, Oklahoma

First Printing 2015

ISBN   978-0-578-17276-7

Lawler Street Book Concern, LLC
Oklahoma City, OK
lawlerstreetbooks@gmail.com

Contents

Preface

These short meditations follow the texts indicated by *The Revised Common Lectionary** for Year C. They were written when the author was pastor of Our Lord's Lutheran Church in Oklahoma City with the intention of encouraging daily Bible reading and prayer at home. Their brevity is due to the limitations of space in the Sunday bulletin. As in the previous book for Year B (*This Week at Home*) the meditations have been grouped according to the seasons of the church year, but because of variations in the calendar and the movable date for Easter, no attempt has been made to assign each reading for a particular day of the year. Spirit led browsing may also be useful. Though it may be an unrealistic expectation, the reader is encouraged to consult the Bible for the full text of each indicated reading.

The author recognizes there are plenty of devotional materials available to Christian readers. These meditations are offered as a testimony with the hope and prayer and they may be of some benefit to the reader's faith in Christ.

--jmf
Willow Creek
Oklahoma City
All Saints Day, 2015

**The Revised Common Lectionary*, © 1992 Consultation on Common Texts.

I. Advent, Christmas and Epiphany

A PRAYER MY MOTHER TAUGHT US
Cause me to hear thy lovingkindness in the morning,
for in thee do I trust.
Cause me to know the way wherein I should walk,
for I lift up my soul unto thee.
Deliver me, O Lord, from my enemies,
I flee unto thee to hide me.
Teach me to do thy will,
for thou art my God;
thy spirit is good;
Lead me into the land of uprightness.

--Psalm 143:8-10, KJV

BEGINNING AT THE END
"People will faint from fear . . ." (Luke 21:25-28; v. 26).
There's nothing like a movie with terrific special effects, or an ominous voice narrating an end-of-the-world scheme on television to fill us with dread and foreboding. The gospel of the Lord Jesus Christ is not about fear. Over against all fear mongers and all the others who spend their lives trying to make sense of "biblical prophecies," the gospel boldly proclaims that, in Jesus, we have nothing to fear. "In the beginning, God . . .;" and in the end, ". . . power and glory"! *For thine is the kingdom and the power and the glory. Forever.*

1

Change

"Heaven and earth will pass away . . ." (Luke 21:29-33; v. 33).
This is nothing new. We all know the earth is changing. Huge, imposing mountains eventually erode into humble outcroppings. The sun, apparently, will run out of energy in a few million years or so. Or did he say "billions"? All of this tells us that our hopes are not tied to creation, but to the Word of God, revealed in Jesus Christ. "The grass withers, the flower falls, but the word of the Lord endures forever" (I Peter 1:24-25). *Lord, keep us steadfast in your Word.*

Instruction

The Lord . . . instructs sinners in the way (Psalm 25; v. 8).
We are satisfied with forgiveness, but God is holding out for transformation. Of course the mercy of God is boundless, and we should never doubt it. And on this side of heaven we will always be "simultaneously justified and sinner" (*simul justus et peccator* in Luther's famous phrase). God forgives, for Jesus' sake, but as we are filled with the grace of the Lord Jesus God also bends and shapes us to conform to the image of Christ. By daily repentance, Old Adam/Eve is drowned, and we are raised as God's new creation (2 Corinthians 5:17). *Teach me the way I should go* (Psalm 143:8).

Holy Hearts

. . . may the Lord make you increase and abound in love . . . and may he strengthen your hearts in holiness (1 Thessalonians 3:9-13; vv.12-13).
Depending on our experiences we may either desire holiness or be repulsed by it. When one is immersed in Scripture and prayer, one might feel holy, or sense 'the Holy,' because of the Word itself. But people who casually mention how much time they spend praying strike us as wanting to show off their holiness. God shows his

2

holiness on the cross where Jesus is "wholly" for us in love. If we "increase and abound in love" it is because we are empowered by the holiness that God creates through the indwelling Holy Spirit. A sanctified heart gives the glory to God. *Holy God, holy mighty, holy immortal, have mercy upon us.* --Orthodox *Trisagion* prayer

TIMING IS EVERYTHING

In those days and at that time . . . (Jeremiah 33:14-16; v. 15).
To our way of thinking God is always slow to act. Faith understands that God always acts "in the fullness of time," at the Right Time, a time known only to God. That "Time" the prophet refers to is the time of Jesus, when God in the flesh shared our life and worked out our salvation through the cross. Sometimes we wait for God. Sometimes, more often perhaps, it is God who waits for us. To those who may be stuck in unhealthy attitudes or behaviors, or a spiritual lethargy of some kind, the Apostle reminds us that "Now is the day of salvation!" (2 Corinthians 6:2). *Thank you, Lord, for the great gift of Time.*

HELD TOGETHER

. . . we pray most earnestly that we may see you face to face and restore what is lacking in your faith (I Thessalonians 3:9-13; v.10).
Face to face is always better. The possibilities of evangelism and Christian nurture through 'social media' notwithstanding, we rejoice to see our friends on Sunday or whatever day of the week we gather for worship or Bible study. The latest news is always interesting, of course, but what really drives our desire to be 'face to face' is that we need to be mutually encouraged and built up in our faith. We may not know it but the person beside us will be comforted immensely when she hears us say the Creed, "I believe in God . . ." In the same way, on another day, we will be held together when the gentleman in the next pew sings, "Praise to the Lord, the Almighty . . ." *I thank you Lord, for the faith of those around me.*

A HEAVY BURDEN

"*. . . weighed down with dissipation and drunkenness and the worries of this life*" (Luke 21:34-36; v. 34).

People who are anxious do not receive the condemnation they deserve! Dissipation and drunkenness are self-destructive behaviors that Jesus censures. In the same breath he includes people "weighed down with . . . the worries of this life." We often take the view that "If I don't worry about my needs, who will?" The answer, of course, is that God knows what we need even before we ask. "Cast all your anxiety on him, because he cares for you" (1 Peter 5:7). *Really, Lord, anxiety is heavy.*

"To pray is to let Jesus come into our hearts."
--Ole Hallesby (1879-1961)

THE WORD RETURNS

The word of God came to John (Luke 3:1-6; v. 2).

There are long dry spells in our lives, when nothing fruitful seems to be happening. God seems distant, or perhaps we are distant from God. We're not sure whether it's a question of unanswered and unheard prayers or simply a lack of desire even to pray. Nevertheless, God's word always returns. As in the days of John the Baptist, so now the purpose of God's word is to lead us to repentance so that we can believe in the One Whom God Sent, Jesus Christ. *Lord God, when I have no words to say, give me ears to hear your word.*

THE REFINERY

He will sit as a refiner and purifier of silver (Malachi 3:1-4; v. 3).

Apparently the refiners of silver in earlier days would draw off the dross until the refiner could see his own image reflected in the molten metal. The image of God is distorted in our lives, hidden under layers of dross and impurities. God is drawing it off, ladle full at a time, until the full image of God's new creation in Christ is reflected in our lives. *Holy Spirit, let the refining fires burn until you like what you see.*

NOT QUITE READY

The one who began a good work among you will bring it to completion by the day of Jesus Christ (Philippians 1:3-11; v. 6).

The elderly Christian gentleman, face perpetually glowing with the inner joy of the Lord Jesus, showed up one day with a badge proclaiming only these initials: P.B.P.W.M.G.I.F.W.M.Y. So of course everyone asked, "OK, Art. What does it mean?" "Please be patient with me; God isn't finished with me yet." We thought Art was already good enough, and more, but the saintly brother in Christ knew better. We all find ourselves at some point along the way to the New Creation promised for those "in Christ" (2 Corinthians 5:17). *Lord Jesus, I thank you for being patient with me.*

PEACE FESTIVAL

Blessed be the Lord God of Israel (Luke 1:68-79; v. 68).

Nearly forgotten in the mad rush toward Christmas is the God of Israel who has not forgotten his original purpose to bring blessing to all nations through Abraham and his descendants. We have allowed the festival of "peace on earth, goodwill to all" to enslave us with an intense anxiety to make everything just perfect. Blessed be God who, in Jesus Christ, "has looked favorably on us" and freed us from every kind of enslavement. *O God, let this be a stress-free Christmas, for Jesus' sake.*

EARLY RISER

The dawn from on high will break upon us (Luke 1:68-79; v. 78).
Sometimes the night goes by too quickly and duty calls. Sometimes the night seems never to end. In any difficulty, anxiety, or need, waiting is always the hardest part. We cannot make the earth turn faster to bring daylight sooner nor can we bend the will of God to our purposes. We have only the promise of redemption through Jesus Christ. We will cling to that in our darkest hours. *My soul waits for you, O Lord; more than watchmen for the morning* (Psalm 130).

SHAREHOLDERS

I thank my God every time I remember you . . . because of your sharing in the gospel . . . (Philippians 1:3-11; vv., 3, 5).
The gospel is meant to be shared, and every Christian is a shareholder. We claim the gospel for ourselves, of course. For Jesus' sake God forgives our sins, frees us from the power of evil, reconciles us with our enemies, and promises life that never ends. The excitement of the gospel builds, however, when we allow God to use us to bring the same message of grace, forgiveness, and life to tortured souls who need it. *There was a time, dear Lord, when I desperately needed your grace. Thank you for sending your messengers.*

HARD WORK

Every valley shall be filled, and every mountain . . . made low (Luke 3:1-6; v. 5).
Highway building is hard work, and expensive, especially if the terrain is hilly or mountainous. The hard work and expensive aspect of getting ready for Christmas has to do with leveling the rough places in our lives and filling in the valleys. Filling in what is missing in a Christian life and witness will without fail surprise us and satisfy us beyond measure. In the same way eliminating things that do not belong in our life could be the liberating experience we

6

have been waiting for. It is the promise of full, free and complete grace of God in Jesus Christ that empowers us to do it. *Give me courage, Lord God, for a bold survey of the hills and valleys in my life.*

SOME SUGGESTIONS

"What then should we do?" (Luke 3:7-18; v. 10).

When the prophet bellows, "Bear fruit worthy of repentance," sometimes we just know what needs to be done. In other circumstances we need a hint. John the Baptist is not stingy with advice. If we are truly sorry and want to wait for the Day of the Lord with clean hearts, the Baptist suggests we can share a coat or share our food. We can refrain from taking advantage of the vulnerable, or abusing the privilege of our office or authority. The fruits of repentance reveal our sincerity, but it is Christ who gives us a clean heart. *First, Lord, let my repentance be sincere.*

THE TRUE SELF

". . . one who is more powerful than I is coming" (Luke 3:7-18; v. 16).

John the Baptist had power to proclaim a message of repentance, to expose hypocrisy, and to rouse the apathetic to action. Jesus has power to forgive and restore life, to expose the image of God engraved in the life of each one of us. Even a life encased in sin and degradation contains, deep down, the kernel that is the true self. Jesus helps us find our God-given self by separating the chaff from the grain. *With all my heart I take refuge in Christ, who restores my true nature.*

A QUALITATIVE DIFFERENCE

. . . the peace of God . . . surpasses all understanding . . . (Philippians 4:4-7; v. 7).

There is a qualitative difference between the world's peace and the peace that Christ leaves with us (John 14:27). The world's peace is

7

always precarious and superficial. The guns are silent for a time, but the enmity persists. There is a sense of well-being but misfortune is potentially around the next corner. Christians are not fooled by the satisfaction generated by good fortune or success. Our peace comes from deep within where God's love in Christ has captured our heart. Even when things are falling apart, we are amazed to find we are at peace, held together by that power called grace. It defies understanding. *Make me an instrument of your peace, O Christ.*

THE SOURCE

With joy you will draw water from the wells of salvation (Isaiah 12:2-6; v.3).
We never outgrow our need for water. When we are thirsty, we have a drink. And when we are thirsty again, we return to the source. Our life of faith also requires frequent refreshment. It would be distressing if water were suddenly unavailable. Thanks be to God, the grace of the Lord Jesus is always available. When our soul dries up, we go back to the Source, Jesus Christ. As weary pilgrims, we gather at the well in joyful anticipation. *Lord Jesus, I thirst.*

THE HARDEST THING

. . . in everything by prayer (Philippians 4:4-7; v. 6).
Prayer is often the last thing we think of. Worry might be the first thing: resentment or frustration might precede "rejoicing always." And prayer may be the hardest thing of all to do today. In the Lord Jesus we discover a God who has already arrived at the place of our joy or frustration or sadness. There, the God revealed in Jesus Christ is waiting for us with the peace that surpasses all understanding. *Lord, I am finally here. Thank you for waiting.*

A SINGING LESSON

Sing aloud . . . with all your heart (Zephaniah 3:14-20; v. 14).

"The LORD has taken away the judgments against you," so there is reason to sing. Whether you have talent, or think you don't, you have a *reason* to sing. If you don't like the songs they sing at church, sing the ones you like at home! You don't remember the words? Make up words that come from your soul! Depending on the day, it could be joyous song or even a sad song. "Above all, sing spiritually. Have an eye to God in every word you sing. Aim at pleasing God more than yourself," was John Wesley's advice. *Thank you, Lord, for the song you have put on my lips today!*

"Music is the heartbeat of God" -- John Ylvisaker

A GOD WHO SINGS

The LORD your God . . . will exalt over you with loud singing (Zephaniah 3:14-20; v. 17).

We know that God speaks ("In the beginning was the Word"). We might not have imagined a God who sings. If angels sing, why wouldn't God sing along? Whether it is the solitary voice of an individual at home, or the voices of men, women and children singing praises with gusto, faces beaming with joy--is not God singing through them and with them? God's love for the human race causes the music to swell up in God's heart, bursting forth in earthly melody and heavenly harmony. Jesus Christ is God's love song to the world. *Gracious God, sometimes I really do hear your song!*

THE WILL OF GOD

"See, I have come to do your will" (Hebrews 10:5-10; v. 9).

It is a battle of wills—our will and God's will. With the mind we align ourselves with God's will, but in the doing our good intentions run into opposition from our own purposes. Finally there is One who with mind and heart and body pours himself into fulfilling God's

9

will for the human race. Jesus Christ came for this, to do God's will, to be the end and fulfillment of the law, so that by his obedience we become righteous. *Take my untamed spirit, Lord Christ, and bend it to your purposes.*

PRECOCIOUS JOY

"The child in my womb leaped for joy" (Luke 1:39-45; v. 44).
The child is John the Baptist who, before he could walk or talk, or even before he was born, recognized the approach of the Holy One. John had a mission and purpose, and so do we. From time to time, as our life situation changes, our purpose and mission might also be modified. But in all cases, Jesus approaches, comes into our lives, teaches us with his grace and directs our actions. Then we leap for joy. *I hear your footsteps, gracious Lord.*

MAGNIFICAT ANIMA MEA

"My soul magnifies the Lord and my spirit rejoices in God my Savior" (Luke 1:46-55; v. 47).
Mary did not need to pray "Come into my heart, Lord Jesus." The Presence of Jesus in her womb was not her idea but Divine Initiative. The Spirit of Jesus has taken the initiative to make a home in our lives as well. We are bound together and to Christ in an intimate fellowship. As Jesus said, "On that day you will know that I am in the Father, and you are in me and I in you" (John 14:20). The miracle of being saved by God's grace causes both body and soul to erupt in praise and rejoicing. *Let it be for me according to your will.*

ALL GENERATIONS

"His mercy is . . . from generation to generation" (Luke 1:46-55; v. 50).
Mary is aware of the universal blessing that follows from the particular event of Jesus' birth. "All generations" will marvel with Blessed Mary who perceived that through her Son God's mercy would extend from "generation to generation." When we sing *Silent*

Night and *Joy to the World* we are joined to generations of those who already lived the wonder of God's salvation in Jesus, as well as with generations yet to come. *Let all the peoples praise you, O God!*

GOD WITH US

The Word became flesh (John 1:1-14; v. 14).

The Word that called light out of darkness and order out of chaos is not an empty echo. God's Word speaks to us still, calling us into life, waiting for our response. God in flesh and bone! God in the hard and soft tissues of daily life, taking on sin, death and devil for our sake. Immanuel: God-with-us, is calling us into his New Creation. *Word Incarnate, a dark and chaotic world awaits your good news.*

CAESAR

. . . a decree . . . (Luke 2:1-20; v. 1).

Caesar's decrees fill mountains of law books. Over and above all human law God also makes a decree. If the human race seems bent on self-destruction, God decrees an end to hatred and vengeance through the forgiveness available in Jesus Christ. If we are ensnared by guilt and the power of sin, God decrees liberation through the death and resurrection of Jesus. If we are beaten down by vile illness, inexplicable tragedy, or the consequences of injustice, God decrees deliverance and final victory through our Lord Jesus Christ. *Sovereign God, I welcome your decrees.*

WHAT WE REALLY NEED

. . . a Savior . . . (Luke 2:1-20; v. 11).

We, who cannot save ourselves, need a Savior. We are caught up and bound in a web of self-deception. We clamor for 'justice' as though we think we know what that really is. Families find themselves repeating harmful behavior driven by deeply rooted attitudes that resist modification. Over against dangers, real or perceived, we look for protection by becoming more dangerous than the perceived threat. We need most of all someone to save us from ourselves! Seeing our deepest need, God has sent his Son, our Lord Jesus Christ, to save us from our insecurities and foolishness and from everything that threatens our well-being before God. *O God, help me to see my need.*

POWER REVEALED IN WEAKNESS
. . . a child . . . (Luke 2:1-20; v. 12)
To redeem humanity and the whole creation from bondage to sin and death might have required the signs in sun and moon that were so widely expected. Instead, "God chose what is weak in the world to shame the strong" (1 Corinthians 1:27). From the "no room in the inn" to the ignominy of the cross, God reveals his power in what we regard as weakness. It is when we are powerless and overcome by life's challenges that the power of God in Jesus Christ can be revealed in our lives as well. *Holy Child of Bethlehem, have mercy upon me.*

CAN'T KEEP FROM SINGING
. . . a multitude . . . (Luke 2:1-20; v. 13).
Heaven and earth could not keep the multitude of God's angels from singing and giving glory to the God who loved us and arranged redemption from bondage to sin and from the consequences of a broken creation. In the same way, the multitudes upon multitudes of all God's redeemed, throughout the ages and into our own lives today cannot be restrained from giving glory and honor to the God who sent his Son into our world. *Dear God, my quivering voice is one among so many, but there is joy in my heart.*

PEACE WITHOUT LIMITS

And on earth peace . . . (Luke 2:1-20; v. 14).

As the spirit of Christmas wraps itself around the world hearts are warmed and hostilities cease. Peace treaties that do not have a mechanism for discharging built up hatred and bitterness will not last long. God's glory that brings peace to earth declares that both the grand disputes of nations as well as the petty claims of individuals are heaped upon the Innocent Child born in Bethlehem. The peace of God in Jesus Christ removes every excuse to hold grudges. *Dear God, help me to see my own grudges, and to let them go, in Jesus' Name.*

A TRUE THESAURUS (*TREASURY*) OF WORDS

Mary treasured all these words . . . (Luke 2:1-20; v. 19).

"Do not be afraid . . . great joy . . . the Messiah is born . . . a child . . . lying in a manger . . . glory to God . . . peace on earth . . ." The greatest birth announcement ever is contained in a few words, barely a paragraph. Yet each word is laden and overflowing with the grace of God. Words that bring us to Jesus, whether they are spoken by angels or by those who care for our livestock, are to be treasured. *I treasure your word in my heart* (Psalm 119:11).

A SONG THAT NEVER GROWS OLD

. . . a new song . . . (Psalm 96; v. 1).

The songs of Christmas tend to be old songs, songs that have been sung for generations past and loved by all in our own time as well. "Heaven and nature" sing with us. The birth of Jesus is good news for the trees of the forest and everything that fills the oceans, as well as for the human race itself. It is a song that is always new and always renewing. Whenever we proclaim Jesus' birth in the words of old songs, the 'glad tidings of great joy' become new all over again. *Lord God, let those who are cheerless find the joy that only you can give.*

THE CONSEQUENCES FOR DISCIPLES
DECEMBER 26: THE FEAST OF STEPHEN

Jerusalem . . . the city that stones . . . those who are sent to it (Matthew 23:34-39; v. 37). Abruptly, on 'the Feast of Stephen,' after contemplating the sheer wonder of God-in-the-flesh, the martyrdom of Stephen leads us to consider the consequences of his birth for those who are disciples. We are not alone in this emotional dislocation. Simeon blessed Mary and said, "A sword will pierce your own soul, too" (Luke 2:35). Just as Jesus grew up to suffer death on the cross, so we, who follow Jesus, are also called to take up the cross and follow him. *Not yet ready for martyrdom, Lord; nevertheless, I follow.*

A LESSON IN PARENTING

Then they started to look for him . . . they returned . . . to search for him . . . (Luke 2:41-52; vv. 44, 45).

If we were unfamiliar with the happy ending, our heightened sense of 'responsible parenting' would leave us appalled to learn that Jesus was without parental supervision for three days! Equally astonishing, for his parents at least, was the claim that his 'Father's house' was really in Jerusalem, instead of Nazareth. It is hard for us to think of anything holier than 'family.' The Boy of Twelve teaches us that, while it is not a good idea to scare our parents, nevertheless our relationship with God is more important than anything else. *Our Father, who art in heaven . . .*

IN JESUS' NAME: PART I

. . . clothe yourselves . . . (Colossians 3:12-17; v. 12).

"Putting on Christ" is a familiar New Testament theme. It is the result of "the Great Exchange" wherein Jesus takes our burdens and makes them his own, and in exchange gives us his righteousness. This takes place in Christ's atoning death and resurrection, and becomes personal for each of us in Baptism. To clothe ourselves with the virtues of Christ—compassion, kindness, humility, meekness and patience—is the baptismal gift. *Lord Jesus, make me comfortable in your righteousness.*

IN JESUS' NAME: PART II

Let the word of Christ dwell in you richly (Colossians 3:12-17; v. 16).

"The word of Christ" refers both to the teaching *of* Jesus and the teaching *about* Jesus. Learning what Christ has done for us (the teaching "about") and learning the way of Christ (the teaching "of") is a life-long process. It happens when we drink deeply in the Word and absorb the message of how God graciously treats us in Jesus. This grace molds and shapes our thoughts and actions, and the gracious way of life that Jesus taught becomes second nature. Or we might say, it becomes our true nature. *Your Word is a lamp to my feet.*

IN JESUS' NAME: PART III

Sing . . . to God . . . (Colossians 3:12-17; v. 16).

This is a word for those who are a bit hesitant to sing in church, for whatever reason. In church we sing to God and for God. It is prayer, communicating with God, and not for show. Certainly not a performance! Your fellow Christians pay no attention to how you sing because they are too absorbed in their own prayer and praise to notice. How you sing is nobody's business. It is your response to the Spirit who communicates God's love to you and instills in you a love for the Lord Jesus Christ. Sing to God, and for God! *Lord God, accept my tonally uncertain joyful noise, in Jesus' Name.*

IN JESUS' NAME: PART IV

. . . do everything in the name of the Lord Jesus (Colossians 3:12-17; v. 17).

Are some deeds too trivial to be undertaken in Jesus' name? Are some conversations too ordinary, too banal, to be conducted in Jesus' name? Tying your shoes in Jesus' name might influence where and how you walk and what people you might meet during the day. Just imagine how ordinary conversation could be transformed into blessing if our end of it were carried out "in Jesus' name"! *It's a struggle to be 'Christian' all the time. I take a deep breath, in Jesus' Name.*

LET THERE BE . . . JOY!

Mountains and all hills, fruit trees and all cedars (Psalm 148; v. 9). "Joy to the earth . . . and heav'n and nature sing" because even "the creation waits with eager longing" (Romans 8:19) for redemption. The Son of God, the Word that said, "Let there be . . ." has become part of creation itself to set us free from captivity to sin and death. Let snow and hail and strong winds and all creatures sing for joy and praise the God who loves us with such intensity. *In my ordinary life, Lord, let there be . . . joy!*

RADIANT FACES

They shall be radiant over the goodness of the LORD (Jeremiah 31:7-14; v. 12).

The grace of the Lord Jesus is most clearly seen when we face adversity or disappointment. When we have an overpowering sense of having failed in our duty, forgiveness brings an inexplicable exuberance. When things do not turn out to our advantage, there is an unseen power that fills us despite the emptiness. When the burden falls heavily or unfairly on our shoulders, by grace serenity takes control. The goodness of the Lord brings radiance to our faces, much to our amazement. *Lord, I pray for a cheerful countenance.*

CHILDREN OF GOD

To all . . . who believed in his name, he gave power to become children of God (John 1:1-13; v. 12).

It may have its problems and eccentricities, but we are always glad to be counted as members of our own family. By faith in the work of Jesus Christ we are made members of God's family, children of the heavenly Father, empowered by the Spirit to hallow our Father's name. The title "No people" no longer applies, but now "Children of the living God" (Hosea 1:9, 10; 1 Peter 2:10). Not merely God's creatures but God's children. It is the Word Made Flesh, crucified, risen and exalted, who makes it possible. *Grant us grace, O God, to call you 'Father,' without embarrassment or equivocation.*

A GRACIOUS GOD

. . . grace and truth came through Jesus Christ (John 1:14-18; v. 17).

In Jesus we learn the true meaning of grace. In Jesus we learn that the truth about God is his graciousness. We fall short of the glory of God, but God brings his glory into our lives. None is righteous, but Christ makes us righteous by his death and resurrection Moses reveals to us our sin and our disposition to rebel against God and in this reveals the truth about ourselves. But Jesus shows us that we have a gracious God, and so reveals the truth about God. *You are the way, the truth and the life, Lord Jesus.*

PRE-APPROVED

He chose us in Christ . . . to be holy and blameless (Ephesians 1:3-14; v. 4).

"You're pre-approved!" is more an invitation to acquire debt than it is good news. Chosen "before the foundation of the world" is an indication of the width and depth of God's love for us. We may not feel holy and blameless, but holy and blameless is what God makes of us in Christ. We do not need a resolution to try harder but an ever deepening awareness of the transforming power of God's grace in Jesus Christ. *O God, I know you think of me before I think of you.*

GOD'S PEOPLE

He destined us for adoption as his children, through Jesus Christ (Ephesians 1:3-14; v. 5).

We were forlorn, longing for that love that knows no limits of height or depth. Then, as though by some inexplicable good fortune, we were adopted as God's sons and daughters. Once we were no people (Hosea 1:9), but now we are God's people (1 Peter 2:10). This was God's plan for us in Jesus Christ. The goodness is not only for us, of course, but for all to whom we can say, 'God has destined you to be his offspring, in Jesus Christ.' *I believe, heavenly Father, that you have set a place for me at your table!*

PRIVILEGED

He declares his word to Jacob . . . his statutes to Israel (Psalm 147:12-20; v. 19).

As people chosen "from before the foundation of the world" we are privileged to know God's word and statutes. If we are familiar with God's word we may take it for granted. Or, like an unexamined treasure, we may even neglect it. The Word of God, Jesus Christ, has been proclaimed to us, given to us, and surrounds us. It is our way of life for forgiveness and salvation. For this reason, the psalmist shouts out: "Praise the Lord!" *Amen and alleluia!*

GOD'S GLORY

So that we . . . might live for the praise of his glory (Ephesians 1:3-14; v. 12).

The glory of God is revealed in Jesus Christ, who became one of us, suffered with and for us, and gave us the victory in the resurrection. It is God's glory to heal enmity between the nations and tribes of the world, to repair broken relationships, and to forgive our individual failures. Our reason to live is to praise these glorious works of God. *Glory to you, our God, glory to you.*

MARKED
You also . . . were marked with the seal of the promised Holy Spirit (Ephesians 1:3-14; v. 13).
"You are mine," says God. In spite of rebellion or simply our disinterest in God, it is God's intention to bring us into fellowship for the renewal and transformation of our lives through Jesus Christ. We can try to hide the seal, or ignore it, but it is always visible to God. God wants to make that seal always visible to us as well. *Yes, Lord, I am yours; in Jesus' Name.*

THE EPIPHANY OF OUR LORD: PART I:
They were overwhelmed with joy (Matthew 2:1-12; v. 10).
The star stopped. They had finally arrived. The Spirit of God somehow gets our attention and creates a restlessness in us until, finally, we arrive at the place of joy. For some, the joy is the awareness of God's unfailing love for all people in all conditions. For others it is release from old attitudes and destructive behaviors. The place to which God leads us is Christ, and for all it is a place of overwhelming joy. *I seem to be always arriving, Lord, and always glad to be here.*

THE EPIPHANY OF OUR LORD: PART II
They knelt down and paid him homage (Matthew 2:1-12; v.11).
From the East they came, and then in waves from North and South and West and East. The nations of the world, on hearing the good news of Jesus Christ, kneel and pay homage to the God-among-us, who bears our burdens and gives us what is His, namely righteousness, innocence, and blessedness. He entered into our

weakness and vulnerability and in Him we conquer sin, death and evil. *I, too, bow and do reverence when I come into your Presence, Lord Jesus.*

THE BAPTISM OF OUR LORD: PART I

He will baptize you with the Holy Spirit . . . (Luke 3:15-22; v. 16).
The word 'baptize' means not only to 'dip, immerse,' but also 'plunge, drench, overwhelm.' Baptism plunges us into the Spirit of Jesus Christ, drenches us with the joy of Jesus. The life-giving power of the cross overwhelms us and is absorbed into every tissue in our body. Through Jesus we belong to God entirely, and the sign of our belonging is the Spirit's presence in us which enables us to call Jesus our 'Lord." *Lord Jesus, you have overwhelmed me with your grace.*

THE BAPTISM OF OUR LORD: PART II

He will baptize you with . . . fire (Luke 3:15-22; v. 16).
Fire is not always a tool for judgment. Fire warms our food and warms our bodies on a cold day. Fire also purifies and cleanses. The role of the Spirit is to 'sanctify,' to make holy. The holy flame of God's Spirit burns away what is not genuine in us, everything that obscures our true nature created in God's image. The fire of the Spirit burns away the chaff and reveals our true self, Christ in us. *This night my soul has caught new fire . . . I feel that heaven is drawing nigher, Glory Hallelujah!* (--Sacred Melodies, 1842).

STIRRED UP

The two went down and prayed for them . . . (Acts 8:14-17; v. 15).
We were baptized in the Name of the Triune God, Father, Son and Holy Spirit. We should never doubt that we have received the Holy Spirit. At Confirmation, we pray that God will "stir up" in us the gift of the Holy Spirit. Peter and John prayed for the Samaritan Christians, and they received the Holy Spirit. It is an act of love when we pray for each other, asking God to give good gifts. When

we ask for good gifts, "How much more will the heavenly Father give the Holy Spirit to those who ask him" (Luke 11:13). *Father in heaven, for Jesus' sake, stir up in* [me] *the gift of your Holy Spirit . . .* (cf. *Lutheran Book of Worship,* p. 201).

A LIFE-CHANGING EVENT
They received the Holy Spirit (Acts 8:14-17; v. 17).
And were they ever surprised! No mere ritual to be performed to satisfy tradition or grandparents, Baptism in the Name of the Triune God is a life-changing event. It is an Act of God in which the power, glory and victory of Christ's death and resurrection become real for us. At Baptism we received the Holy Spirit. Empowered now to take up the cross, redeemed from sin's dominion and death's finality, the Spirit surprises us with the joy of Jesus in our hearts and lives. *Lord Jesus, raise me again to newness of life.*

DIVINE SERVICE
In his temple all say, "Glory!" (Psalm 29; v. 9).
The idea of worship is well summarized in this word, Glory! Hearts full of thanksgiving and amazement at God's work in our lives— sustaining, forgiving, transforming—evoke a cry of "Glory!" Then, in worship, which used to be called "Divine Service," we see that it is God who comes into our presence in Word and Sacrament, having become our Servant in Jesus Christ. Then thanksgiving and amazement are compounded and the cries of "Glory!" echo and resound forever. *Glory and Hallelujah and Amen and Amen!*

NAMING
I have called you by name, you are mine (Isaiah 43:1-7; v. 1).
From time to time there are impediments to our relationship with God. Fear, anger, or disappointment might lead us to question God's commitment. Often it is our own behavior that creates a barrier to our happiness before God. It is God who seeks to restore

communion. "Do not fear! I have called you by name." At Baptism our name is intimately and forever connected with the Name of God. "You are mine" is God's promise to us through Jesus Christ. *And I am yours, Lord God; in Jesus' Name.*

FULLY ALIVE

. . . my sons . . . and my daughters . . . whom I created for my glory (Isaiah 43:1-7; vv. 6,7).

Parents glory in being with their children and watching them in their activities. God also takes pleasure in our company and in seeing how our lives are fulfilled in using the gifts that God has given us. Irenaeus (ca. 150 AD) said, "The glory of God is the human being fully alive." Through Jesus Christ, the Beloved Son, we come alive as God's beloved sons and daughters. *Father in heaven, hallowed be thy name.*

MY TEACHER is Jesus Christ; my food is Jesus Christ; the source of my actions is Jesus Christ. —Coptic monk

---

JESUS IS LORD

. . . no one can say "Jesus is Lord" except by the Holy Spirit (1 Corinthians 12:1-11; v. 3).

Outbursts of spiritual energy in this or that group of Christians are taken as signs that the Holy Spirit is up to something powerful and exciting *there, among them!* Others look on with apprehension as though they have been left out. Here is the plainest reassurance. If we are able to say, without gagging on the words, "Jesus is Lord," it is an unmistakable sign that we, too, have been endowed with the Holy Spirit. All that is lacking then is to live believing the truth of our confession and embracing the consequences. *Dear Lord Jesus: sometimes, enough said.*

MARY, MOTHER OF OUR LORD

"Do whatever he tells you" (John 2:1-11; v. 5).

Jesus does not seem to be ready to be fully engaged in his work and ministry. "My hour has not yet come." A wedding reception did not seem to be the right time or place. Or was it? Sometimes we would like to turn off our Christianity, go off duty, and just be, without responsibility or purpose. Mary, the Mother of Our Lord, who is good at pondering things in her heart, is also the activist. In season and out of season, the time is always right for obedience to the word of our Lord and Savior Jesus Christ. *Lord Christ, help me to hear and obey what you command, always.*

IN OUR FATHER'S HOUSE

They feast on the abundance of your house (Psalm 36; v 8).

The relatives are happy to let a rich brother-in-law whose house always has plenty of meat and drink be the perpetual host of every family barbecue. In the same way, our generous God welcomes us with open arms. There are only delicious things on God's table: forgiveness and peace and joy in God's house forever and ever. *Heavenly Father, may I never miss supper in your house.*

HEART POUNDING EXCITEMENT

You shall be a crown of beauty in the hand of the LORD (Isaiah 62:1-5; v.3).

Enough of low self-esteem! For Jesus' sake, God turns unworthy people into a crown of beauty. "As the bridegroom rejoices over the bride, so shall your God rejoice over you" (v. 5). The heart pounds excitedly when the beloved comes into view. In the same way, when we come into God's presence, day by day, through Scripture and prayer, God is thrilled to see us. *It is amazing to find myself in your Presence, dear God.*

23

GOING THROUGH THE MOTIONS

"Now draw some out" (John 2:1-11; v. 8).

Christians sometimes experience an emptiness. Our prayers do not move us or change the things we pray for. Difficult people seem impervious to our Christian charm. It is often hard to see the results of our witness. The jars of water are full, but to what purpose? Now draw some out, Jesus says. Even though you feel you are just going through the motions, nevertheless, draw some out. Let obedience to the command of Jesus be our incentive and its own reward, and let the Lord Jesus give whatever signs serve his purpose. *Fill my impoverished spirit, Lord God, with the grace of Jesus Christ.*

GIFTS WITHOUT LIMITS

. . . varieties of gifts . . . services . . activities. . . (1 Corinthians 12:1-11; vv. 4, 5).

Just as there seems to be infinite creativity in the formation of snowflakes, so the Spirit of God is without limits in distributing the characteristics necessary for the life of the church, the Body of Christ. For some reason (God's joyful creativity, probably!) we cannot all be alike, but each one is unique for the purpose of contributing to the common good. The gifts, services and activities that come naturally to us are manifestations that the Holy Spirit is really at work in our midst, for the sake of the gospel of Jesus Christ. *Holy Spirit, help me to discern the gifts you have given me, and not be afraid to use them, for Jesus' sake.*

JOY

The joy of the LORD is your strength (Nehemiah 8:1-10; v. 10).

How quickly things we count on can crumble and we are left looking at the dust. A natural disaster, a financial crisis, and suddenly plans change against our will. Even on ordinary days, our to-do list is never accomplished. We have expectations for ourselves that we cannot live up to, much less to what God hopes and expects from us.

In all of this, when foundations are shaken, when we deal with disappointments for whatever reason, what is left is the grace of God in Jesus Christ. This is the source of inexplicable joy and the power to carry on. *Dear God, I am trading in my sullen spirit for the joy of the Lord.*

SWEETER THAN HONEY

The law of the Lord is . . . sweeter than honey . . . (Psalm 19; v. 7).
Our human instincts lead us to rebel against God's law, but when we dare to taste it, we see that the Lord is good indeed, and God's desire to embrace us is sweeter than even life itself. Some fear submission to the law of the Lord, but through the Covenant God issues an appeal for fellowship and communion, an invitation to peace in our hearts and gladness in our souls. It is in Jesus, the fulfillment of the law, where we experience God's sweetness most intensely. *Lord, teach this rebellious heart to love your law.*

THE INDISPENSABLE ONES

. . . those who seem to be weaker are indispensable . . .
(1 Corinthians 12:21-31; v. 22).
There is no one who is unneeded in the body of Christ, the Church. Nor are there "weaker" members—only those who "seem" to be weaker. God has a purpose and a role for all Christian people, old and young, boisterous and quiet, whether they show up or not. Everyone has gifts from God to contribute "for the common good," so that through these gifts all may experience the presence of the Lord Jesus Christ in real life. *I am thankful that in some way or another I am needed.*

THE TEACHER

He began to teach in their synagogues (Luke 4:14-21; v. 15).
Jesus is our teacher, and we have much to learn, and even much to unlearn. Old habits and attitudes, both conventional wisdom and our own idiosyncratic wisdom, are all challenged when Jesus sits down

to teach us. It requires a dose of courage to listen to Jesus. There is, however, his promise. "Take my yoke upon you and learn from me . . . and you will find rest for your souls" (Matthew 11:29). *Teacher, help me to release the old burdens in order to be yoked to you.*

THIRSTY

The scribe Ezra . . . read it . . . from early morning until midday (Nehemiah 8:1-3; v. 3).

After we have wandered aimlessly for a while, losing our bearings, we long for the refreshment of God's word. For some the thirst for a word from God is so great they will listen from early morning until noon. Even if we take the word in smaller doses, our lives take on new meaning and direction when we are oriented to God's word, the Word made flesh, Jesus Christ. *Gracious God, let me never be found yawning at your word.*

TOUGH LOVE

Love . . . bears all things, believes . . . hopes . . . endures all things (1 Corinthians 13:1-13; v. 7).

This is the original 'tough love.' Believing and hoping, love has little to go on, except the Spirit's urging and the Resurrection's empowerment. In bearing and enduring 'all things,' love may not find much encouragement. Such love cannot be imposed as a rule or norm, because it is learned in fellowship with Christ. The love that hopes and endures is not expected of anyone who has not been taken up into the love of the Lord Jesus Christ. In Christ, many have found themselves capable of great endurance. *O God, help me to love my neighbor as myself; in Jesus' Name.*

THE LIBERATOR

" . . . release to the captives . . . fulfilled . . . " (Luke 4:14-21; vv. 18, 21).

When the Lord Jesus announces that we are free, we are free indeed. Sins are forgiven, really and absolutely, in Jesus' name. When Jesus announces freedom in our hearing, it means attitudes and habits that alienate us from God and from our neighbor are unbound. Jesus announces the fulfillment of God's word, and in our hearing he frees us from all other captivities and allegiances so that we belong to Christ alone. As it was in the beginning, so now, Jesus speaks, and it is done! *Let your word of freedom thunder and echo in my soul, Lord Jesus.*

GOD'S PLAN

. . . my words . . . to destroy . . . and to plant (Jeremiah 1:4-10; vv. 9, 10).

When God's word pleases us, we praise the messenger. When God's word shows us where we have fallen short of the glory of God, we would like to push the prophet over the cliff. Sometimes old buildings cannot be saved and must be torn down to make room for the new. God's plan in Jesus Christ, even if it involves judgment, is to promote new life with God and well-being with our neighbors. *O God, break through my stubbornness and raise me, with Christ, to newness of life.*

THE PRESENTATION OF OUR LORD
FEBRUARY 2

She began to speak about the child . . . (Luke 2:22-40; v. 38).

Every person's experience of Jesus is unique. Ancient Anna told people that this Child has to do with "the redemption of Jerusalem." Simeon saw Jesus as "a light to the Gentiles." Another might experience Jesus as "the love that will not let me go." Someone else might know Jesus as the One who restores my true nature. *Lord Jesus, you are many things to different people, and your grace is perfect for each one.*

CAST OFFS

Do not cast me off in the time of old age (Psalm 71; v. 9).

The end of life can be difficult. That is not good news and nothing to look forward to, but we know it is the truth. Martin Luther thought the great temptation for old age was despair. The psalmist verges on despair in this antiphon, "Do not cast me off . . . even to old age and gray hairs" (v. 18). In our final infirmity, whether short or prolonged, we should know that the God who took us from our mother's womb promises that life, not death, is his definitive word to us through Jesus Christ. *Dear God, I am counting the days, and thankful for each one.*

RIDDLES

Now we see in a mirror dimly (1 Corinthians 13:1-13; v. 12).

Life does not always give us the answers we were looking for, and we may not even be asking the right questions. Whence this madness of bloodletting between sect and sect and clan and clan? Why is illness so capricious, striking here but not there? Why is my life harder than his? We look in the mirror and see only riddles. God's promise has always been about *the Then! On that Day!* On that Day! the victory of Jesus over sin, death and evil will be revealed, and we finally will see face to face. *Thy kingdom come, heavenly Father!*

RAGE

. . . all were filled with rage (Luke 4:21-30; v. 28).

Jesus was pointing out that the compassion of God extends even to people who are not members of our community, even to people not of our religion, or even of our nationality! And on hearing this, the people were filled with rage. There is no shortage of rage in our world today directed against people who are of a different religion or nationality. Sometimes we are very close to throwing someone over the cliff. Jesus walked away from their rage and went his way. The indwelling Spirit of Jesus allows us to leave rage, theirs and ours, there at the edge of the cliff. *It seems almost too much to ask, dear God, to turn our rage into love.*

RATED 'R'

Christ died for our sins in accordance with the scriptures (1 Corinthians 15:1-11; v. 3).

Telling the gospel is not as hard as we make it out to be. Even children learn to say, "Christ died for our sins." Of course, believing that we need a Savior is hard for some people to accept. There is nothing pretty about the cross—depictions of the suffering of Jesus will always be rated 'R' for violence—but shining through the gruesomeness of the crucifixion is God's self-sacrificing love for us, and the freedom from the power of sin and death that is ours through faith in Christ. *Let your face shine upon our need, gracious Lord.*

THE RIGHT EQUIPMENT

The fishermen . . . were washing their nets (Luke 5:1-11; v. 2).

Good workers always take care of their equipment. Peter and the other candidates for discipleship were getting their nets ready before hanging them up to dry. Tools for faithful Christian discipleship include paying prayerful attention to the Word, being nourished at the Lord's Table, and recalling daily the baptismal gift. Then, *"Master, if you say so, I will let down the nets."*

HOLINESS

This has touched your lips (Isaiah 6:1-8; v. 7).

Isaiah saw the holiness that we can only imagine. So let us imagine it! Here we are, before the Holy, Holier, Holiest One, and we recognize that we do not belong here. Our lips and minds, thoughts and deeds are conditioned by our humanity, and unworthy of occupying a place in the Divine Presence. Nevertheless, God's power and glory reaches out and touches us. At the Lord's Table, that burning you feel in your stomach is Jesus Christ Himself who declares us righteous. *Lord, turn my 'Woe is me' into 'Here I am; send me.'*

GOD'S HANDS

Do not forsake the work of your hands (Psalm 138; v. 8).

We like to think that we are our own best work. We have fashioned a career trajectory and made plans for a perfectly fulfilled life. Perhaps God also has plans for us. As baptized disciples of the Lord Jesus, we are not our own. By the cross of Jesus we belong to God, and God intends to use us as instruments of grace and righteousness, just exactly where we live and work. "I am confident . . . that the one who began a good work among you will bring it to completion by the day of Jesus Christ." (Philippians 1:6). *Make me an instrument of your peace.*

TODAY, BY GRACE

By the grace of God I am what I am (1 Corinthians 15:1-11; v. 10).

It is not, "By grace I still am what I used to be." Rather, God has taken a sinful, corrupt, rebellious and disobedient individual and made me into something new. If anyone is in Christ, there is a new creation (2 Corinthians 5:17). Neither are we yet what we shall be (1 John 3:2). Today by grace, I am what God has made me. *You are the potter, I am the clay.*

THE PRESENCE OF GOD

"Do not be afraid . . ." (Luke 5:1-11; v. 10).

The presence of the Holy One, Jesus Christ, Son of God, in our lives may cause us to say, "Go away from me, for I am sinful person." The angels in the Bethlehem field, the angel at the empty tomb, and Jesus in the boat all affirm that the Presence of God is not for condemnation but for salvation, joy, victory, and freedom from sin, death, and the power of evil. *Nevertheless, in your Presence I am always awestruck.*

HONESTY BEFORE GOD

The heart is devious above all else (Jeremiah 17:5-10; v. 9).

The easiest person to fool is one's self, and we do it all the time. In an instant we can think of many reasons to justify our actions or inactions. God, of course, is never fooled. Honesty is always the best policy, especially before God. Rather than cover up or explain away our failures, it is better to acknowledge our true motives and rely on the grace of the Lord Jesus to forgive the past and to empower us for courageous discipleship today and tomorrow. *Lord Jesus, I confess sometimes even my true motives are hidden from me.*

NOT IN VAIN

. . . in vain . . . in vain . . . futile . . . pitied (1 Corinthians 15:12-20; vv. 14, 17, 19).

Faith lives on the razor's edge between doubt and assurance, between admiration and ridicule. Though we often peer into the bottomless chasm of doubt, the persistent proclamation that "Christ is risen!" pulls us back, time and again. By faith in the risen Christ, we believe that our life and work as Christians is not in vain but represents the seed bearing the promise of life in all its fullness. *Holy Spirit, blow the dark clouds away and renew me in faith, hope and love.*

PRODUCTIVITY

Happy are those who do not . . . sit in the seat of scoffers (Psalm 1; v. 1).

Those who sit at the city gate watching the comings and goings of Christian people may find our willingness to live sacrificially as weakness, our hope of resurrection absurd, our eagerness to forgive foolish. Nevertheless, drawing the waters of the Lord's grace up into our roots, we discover that it is vengeance and selfishness that dry out the soul, and forgiveness and service that produce the flowers

31

and fruit. *Lord God, please silence that nagging voice from within that discourages discipleship.*

RESURRECTION OF THE BODY
Christ has been raised from the dead (1 Corinthians 15:12-20; v. 20)
Who can say or even imagine what our resurrected body will look like? The continuity and difference between our present body and the resurrection body may be something like the relation between seed and flower. Looking at the seed no one could imagine the flower. God has promised resurrection, and the resurrection of Jesus is the power, pledge and sign of something beyond imagination. Nevertheless, we grasp the promise for ourselves and for those who have already 'fallen asleep.' If there is any doubt, let us gather on the next Lord's Day to confess, "We believe in the resurrection of the body, and the life everlasting." *O God, against the scoffers, I pray for courage to believe in the promised resurrection.*

BLESSING
"Blessed are you who are poor . . . hungry . . . who weep" (Luke 6:17-26; vv. 20, 21).
God's promise of blessing still rests upon those who are physically poor and hungry and sad. God values human life in all its aspects— the joy of eating, the comfort of a home, the love of a family. When we embrace the poor, the hungry, and those who are sad, we share in God's mission, revealed in the human body of his Son, Jesus Christ. *Lord Jesus, give me eyes to see you in my neighbor's need.*

EXODUS
They . . . were speaking of his departure (Luke 9:28-36; v. 31).
"Departure" (literally 'exodus') doesn't seem so drastic, until we realize it refers to Jesus' death. Back from the glorious retreat on the mountain top we have been joined to this New Exodus and are on the way to the cross. Our Red Sea is baptism where we die with

Christ and are raised with him to newness of life. The glory of the new creation however, cannot be experienced without the cross. *"The old person in us with all sins and evil desires is to be drowned through daily sorrow for sin . . ."* (Luther's *Small Catechism*).

TRANSFORMATION

All of us . . . are being transformed . . . (2 Corinthians 3:12-4:2; v. 18).

As Jesus was *transfigured* on the mountain, so we Christians are being *transformed* into the image of Christ, day by day, from glory to glory. When we look in the mirror the image reflected back is the image of Christ in us. If the image is one of suffering or anguish, it is Christ crucified suffering with us. If it is one of joy, it is the indwelling exalted Christ. If it is the image of one with work to do, it is Christ the Servant who has given us a 'ministry,' a service to be performed. *Glory to you, O God, for the gift of transformation.*

SHARING, BUT NOT TOO MUCH

. . . they kept silent . . . (Luke 9:28-36; v. 36).

We do not need to share every spiritual experience. If it is an ecstatic experience, the others will be jealous, and if it is an experience of the barren desert others may not even want to hear about it. At the right time the disciples shared the mountaintop experience, not for personal aggrandizement but to witness to the glory of Jesus Christ. Stories of one's own 'faith journey' are sometimes interesting, but not always pertinent to the story of Jesus. *In the peaks and valleys of my journey, your grace is always constant and sufficient.*

II. Lent

O Christ, Thou Lamb of God,
that takest away the sin of the world,
have mercy upon us . . .
grant us thy peace.

ASH WEDNESDAY

You desire truth . . . (Psalm 51; v. 6).

With God there can only be complete honesty. We can fool ourselves with rationalizations and excuses, but "God is not mocked" (Galatians 6:7). God is also completely honest and faithful with us. In answer to our truth God forgives and makes us truly alive. On Ash Wednesday we acknowledge this truth: "Remember that you are dust." We are able to do this because God remembers (Psalm 103:14), and Easter is our hope and promise. *Gracious God, I pray that my painful truth may be healed by the cross of Christ.*

GOD CARES

The LORD heard our voice and saw our affliction, our toil, and our oppression (Deuteronomy 26:1-11; v. 7).

We should never think that 'no one cares.' God sees and cares deeply about us, especially when we are weighed down with affliction and overwhelming tasks. The sign of God's caring is the cross. God has made our suffering his own, and just when we thought we couldn't bear it anymore, the wind blows, the sea opens before us, and it is the day of deliverance. *Just knowing you see me, Lord, enables me to carry on.*

TOO MUCH

The word is near you, on your lips and in your heart (Romans 10:8-13; v. 8).

The word of God that saves, rescues, gives joy and gladness is the name of Jesus Christ, Son of God, our Savior. Under the burden of too much work, too much worry, too much guilt, the word that comes to us and brings us into the joy of the Lord is the name 'Jesus', on our lips and in our hearts. *Jesus . . .*

GOD'S MESSENGERS

He will command his angels . . . to guard you in all your ways (Psalm 91; v. 11).

We do not need to look for the wings, only the blessings. Sometimes angels are visible and sometimes invisible. Most of the time we do not recognize their presence and aid. But always God's messengers are around us to encourage, mentor, help and comfort us, however desperate our need. If we pay attention, God's angels will protect us from our own foolishness. *There I was, alone, and you sent help.*

WE SUSPECTED AS MUCH

The devil said, "To you I will give their glory and all this authority" (Luke 4:1-13; v. 6).

This is dreadful news. The power to give the kingdoms of the world "to anyone I please" is in the hands of the devil. It is awful news, but it doesn't really surprise us. We suspected as much all along. Power in the hands of the wrong people is demonic. The salvation for us is the same as it was for Jesus. Worship—not the nation or a leader, and neither power nor the powerful—but "worship the Lord your God and serve only him." *Help me, Lord God, to recognize the idols in my life.*

DAILY BREAD

One does not live by bread alone (Luke 4:1-13; v. 4).

The hidden discipline of fasting teaches that there is more to life than bread. Food is important. It is God's gift and God wants to give it to all people. That is why we pray for 'daily bread,' and that is why we take up offerings for food banks. Sometimes those who have too much food need to give it up for a time in order to discover the One from whom all blessings flow, the God who gives us all things through Jesus Christ. *Help me never to value the gift more than the Giver, Lord God.*

PLUNGING HEADFIRST

"Do not put the Lord your God to the test (Luke 4:1-13; v. 12).

The protective grace of God is not an invitation to foolishness or rash behavior, or even to test the limits of Christian freedom. The risk Jesus calls us to is not dangerous living—physically or morally—but the risk of plunging headfirst into a life of service to God and love for neighbor. While the world and the devil mock us, we will find ourselves supported and surrounded by the angels. *Lord Jesus, help me to live dangerously, in the right way.*

AT THE DOOR

. . . until an opportune time (Luke 4:1-13; v. 13).

Discussions about the devil usually miss the point. Our problem is not how to picture the devil but how to recognize temptation when it comes. "Sin is lurking at the door; its desire is for you" (Genesis 4:7). Temptation comes when we least expect it, maybe even while sitting in church. For us the "opportune time" is often when we are convinced of our own righteousness. "If you think you are standing, watch out that you do not fall" (1 Corinthians 10:12). For Christians, the most powerful temptation is to flee from the cross of discipleship. *Help me to be more clever than the tempter!*

COUNTING STARS

. . . he believed the LORD (Genesis 15:1-6; v. 6).

Count the stars, Abraham was told. So shall your descendants be. At that point Abraham couldn't even count one heir. Nevertheless, against all sense and reason, Abraham believed the Lord. Against a nagging conscience; against all feelings of unsatisfied need; against our inability to see any positive outcome at all, nevertheless we believe that God will satisfy all our needs though Jesus Christ. When doubts and questions plague our soul, it is stars we count, not sheep. *I praise you, O God, for the outcomes I cannot yet see.*

SAFETY LAST

"I must be on my way" (Luke 13:31-35; v. 33).

Jesus is going head first into the place where he is least safe. Safety, comfort, rest—these are the things we most want from God, and they may be what we least need. Christian commitment is lived in the company of Jesus, and Jesus is going to Jerusalem, the place of self-offering in love for the world. Christian love is usually realized in places where there is neither safety, nor comfort, nor rest. *Lord Jesus Christ, may your way be my way as well.*

FORSAKEN

If my father and mother forsake me, the LORD will take me up (Psalm 27; v. 10).

The truth is that there will be times when we experience forsakenness, real or perceived. The fall onto the hard floor is painful. Parents cannot promise their children that bad things won't happen. We have no promise that the reality of Christian life will be free from pain and suffering. The promise is that the One who experienced absolute forsakenness on the cross, Jesus Christ, will be in that place of suffering, to "take us up" into his grace and mercy. *I thank you, Lord Christ, that you are 'in my place' today.*

CITIZENS OF ANOTHER PLACE

Our citizenship is in heaven (Philippians 3:17-4:1; v. 20).

"Worship the Lord your God and serve only him" Jesus said to the devil. In the Bible there are no degrees of worship or loyalty beyond the first and only priority: God alone is worthy of worship. We are thankful for the places where God has brought us to live in this world, for language and culture and local traditions that make life interesting. We pray for the welfare of our city, to be sure (Jeremiah 29:7), and we work for justice and the common good. But as Christians we have one citizenship, and that is as members, by grace, of God's kingdom, where Jesus is our Lord. *Preserve me from every kind of idolatry, Lord God.*

FELLOWSHIP

. . . whom I love and long for . . . (Philippians 3:17-4:1; v. 1).

The hermitage was not for the Apostle Paul. He needed Christian fellowship, especially when that fellowship was unavailable by distance or by incarceration in a Roman jail. It is not merely human contact that we desire—one can go to the mall and bump into lots of people. It is contact with people who share our faith in the crucified and risen Lord Jesus Christ that we long for with all our heart. *Dear God, I am always encouraged to be with other Christians.*

EVEN THE ANGRY

"Jerusalem, Jerusalem . . ." (Luke 13:31-35; v. 34).

The city or land or individual who refuses to attend to God's call will finally collapse into violence and bloodshed. It is God's will to gather together, "like a hen gathers her brood under her wings," all people—even those who have been angry with each other—into forgiving fellowship in the Lord Jesus Christ. *By your Spirit, heavenly Father, may all nations hear the gracious call of our Lord Jesus.*

HOSANNA!

Blessed is the one who comes in the name of the Lord (Luke 13:3-35; v.35).

Finally, there is a commotion at the city's edge. Our heads and hearts turn away from petty quarrels and finite concerns to hail the One who comes to take away the sin of the world, to conquer death and devil, to establish the peaceful kingdom where all are caught up in God's loving embrace. We cry out Hosanna! And the cry echoes throughout ages and ages. *You are passing by, Lord Jesus, and I bow my head in reverent adoration.*

INSEPARABLE

"I have come looking for fruit on this fig tree, and still I find none (Luke 13:6-9; v. 7).

There are some things that cannot be separated. For example, Law and Gospel: you can't understand one without the other. Or, Sin and Grace—these are realities that need to be understood together. And there is another inseparable pair: hearing and doing, faith and fruit, belief and works. Jesus said, "I appointed you to go and bear fruit, fruit that will last" (John 15:16). *O God, help me to love the reality of good works as much as I love the idea of faith.*

NOT FINISHED

"Why should it be wasting the soil?" (Luke 13:6-9; v. 7).

The barren tree could very well be uprooted and replaced with another tree, or maybe with a bed full of wildly blooming flowers. Let us raise our voice in protest. "No! We're not finished. Look, the sap is still flowing. Come, Holy Spirit! Let there be new life, new growth, in my life of faith, and let the fruits of the Spirit dangle from my branches to bring blessing in Jesus' name." *Amen! Come, Holy Spirit!*

LATE BLOOMERS
"Sir, let it alone for one more year . . ." (Luke 13:6-9; v. 8).
Some trees are slow to bloom, and so are some people. Let us pray for a sudden rush of flowers and fruits among us, so that those who are hungering and thirsting for the organic food of the gospel of Jesus Christ may be satisfied. "The fruit of the Spirit is love, joy, peace, patience, kindness, generosity, faithfulness, gentleness, and self-control" (Galatians 6:22). *You, O God, are the fertile soil; let me be a fruitful tree.*

A DRINK OF WATER
O God . . . my soul thirsts for you . . . (Psalm 63; v. 1).
Nutritionists tell us that when we feel like a snack maybe we just need a drink of water. In the same way, if we sense a vague anxiety in our life and are not sure where it comes from, maybe we just need God. Saint Augustine wrote, *"O God, thou hast made us for thyself and our hearts are restless till they find their rest in thee."*

MANAGEMENT
For you have been my help (Psalm 63; v. 7).
We've had close calls. We have been perplexed. We have suffered deep disappointments, even tragedies. Yet here we are, sustained and led by invisible hands, encouraged in wondrous ways, and we open our eyes to discover we are still intact. "How did you manage?" they ask. And we say, "It was not I who managed, but God who managed me." *". . . and so, in the shadow of your wings, I sing for joy."*

ENOUGH
Why do you spend your money for that which is not bread? (Isaiah 55:1-9; v. 2).
Garage sales bear witness to money spent for that which is not bread. If, in answer to our prayers for "daily bread," God provides the

means to acquire it, then we recognize that our money is not really ours but God's. How we spend our money then becomes a stewardship issue, and we are accountable to God. Our thirst for more and more cannot be satisfied at any price. What we really need God gives us by grace, through Jesus Christ. *Lord, help me to know when to say 'Enough.'*

THE THOUGHT OF GOD
For my thoughts are not your thoughts . . . says the LORD (Isaiah 55:1-9; v. 8).
Who would presume to say what is on God's mind? Yet we all would like to think that we are on God's side and that our thoughts coincide perfectly with God's plans and ideas. The chief Thought of God is Jesus Christ, the Word made flesh. It is God's idea to give us life through the suffering and death of the beloved Son. Suffering and struggles cast us into the mystery of what God is doing in our lives and in our world. We can only listen and trust that somehow the Thought of God is working for our good, to bring us to life in God's Presence. *Who speaks for you, O God, except your Son, Jesus Christ?*

HOMECOMING
I will get up and go to my father . . . (Luke 15:11-19; v. 18).
We all have to swallow our pride from time to time when we realize we have done something foolish. The One who covers our shame, forgives our sin, and who doesn't hold us up to contempt is God our Father. For Jesus' sake, and at his invitation, the door is always open, and the welcome is always warm. When we come to our senses, the Spirit points us in the direction of our true home. *You are a hiding place for me* (Psalm 32:7).

FEELING BETTER

Father, I have sinned against heaven and before you (Luke 15:11-24; v. 21).

Down in the mud, jostling the hogs for a place at the trough, is not a healthy place to be. Unacknowledged and unconfessed sin will always take its toll, and we will always feel better when we open up before God to tell the truth. It is a loving and forgiving God who hears the cry of the penitent. For Jesus Christ's sake God pulls us up, washes us off, and restores our dignity *While I kept silence, my body wasted away* (Psalm 32:3).

FORGIVENESS

While I kept silence, my body wasted away (Psalm 32; v. 3).

The full and open confession of sin is not a plea bargain, wherein the guilty one looks for a lesser punishment. Before God confession is for forgiveness, not judgment! When we try to hide the truth from God our own conscience eats away at us. When we open ourselves to God "from whom no secrets are hid" we experience cleansing, healing, and full forgiveness of sin, for Jesus Christ's sake. *Lord, where should I begin? I'll begin at the beginning.*

TRUE PLEASURE

Quickly, bring out a robe—the best one . . . (Luke15:20-24; v. 22).

There was no bargaining, no negotiating, between father and son. The confession made, the sin was forgiven. The lost son was found and clothed with the best robe in the house. Wrapped in the righteousness of Christ, the Father in heaven beams with joy. Redeemed from evil's power, we cannot help it if a silly, self-conscious grin of pleasure sneaks across our face. *You forgave the guilt of my sin* (Psalm 32:5).

THE HAPPY EXCHANGE

For our sake he made him to be sin . . . so that in him we might become the righteousness of God (2 Corinthians 5:16-21; v. 21).

Luther called this the 'happy exchange.' Sin is not so much the sum of individual acts (sins) as it is a state of being deep within our souls

43

that cries out for redemption. Jesus became sin, which means that, before Christ has his way with us, *we are* sin. When Christ initiates the happy exchange, *we are* God's righteousness. Our souls are cleansed and reborn and God's righteousness is at work in the world through us. *Spirit of God, help me to come to terms with this new arrangement.*

THE ELDER SON
Son, you are always with me, and all that is mine is yours (Luke 15:25-32; v. 31).
The elder son comes from the field in his work clothes and casts a cloud on the general happiness in the house. The one gained nothing by running away, and the other lost nothing when the Father rejoiced at the lost son's return. The parable ends abruptly. The question is whether life-long obedience will result in self-centered resentment or in joy and love for the rescued. *Steadfast love surrounds those who trust in you, O LORD.*

THE ANNUNCIATION OF OUR LORD
MARCH 25
Nothing will be impossible for God (Luke 1:26-38; v. 37).
Our first thought is usually to raise objections. There is a plan, a proposal, an idea, but just as quickly there are all kinds of reasons why it should not be considered. Scripture is full of impossible plans—Abraham and Sarah, Hannah, David vs. Goliath, Mary, the Cross! If God chooses to use us, unimpressive as we may be, to be instruments of God's grace, power and love, what can we say except *"Here am I, the servant of the Lord; let it be with me according to your word."*

THE WAY IN THE WILDERNESS
I will make a way in the wilderness (Isaiah 43:16-21; v. 19).
We may have the idea that God is found only in the green pastures and the still waters. We need to be assured that God is with us in the

wilderness as well. In fact, when life is toughest and adversity bears down it is God who is walking beside us, and ahead of us, making a way through it all. The chief sign of God's presence in the wilderness is the cross, and the Way in the wilderness is Jesus Christ. *Thank you, Lord, for the wilderness. It is where I learn the meaning of faith.*

KNOWING CHRIST
I want to know Christ (Philippians 3:4b-14; v. 10).
We do not need to sit down with Jesus for coffee and a long conversation to discover the mind, will and purpose of Christ. We need merely claim the baptismal promise of death and resurrection, walk with him in the way of the cross, follow him as he empties himself of all divine privileges and honors and becomes our servant. If we need more clarity into the mind of Christ, if we need encouragement to pick up our own cross, he invites us to his Table for the Bread of Life. *Lord Jesus, when I find myself in the shadow of the cross let me know also the power of your resurrection.*

If you know Christ well, it is enough, even if you know nothing else; if you do not know Christ it is nothing, even if you learn all else.
–Life motto of Luther's friend Johannes Bugenhagen.

DREAMERS
We were like those who dream (Psalm 126; v. 1).
Dreams may be the first to go when we are in the wilderness. The heat, the sweat, the sore feet and tired legs constrain and confuse our vision. Both dream and fulfilment are God's gifts. The dream of an earth of justice, peace, and well-being among all people is godly and Spirit-generated. The Spirit also leads us to believe that Jesus Christ is the fulfilment of God's dream for us and the world. Living the gospel life of forgiveness and service, they will ask: Is it a dream or

is it real? The answer is 'Yes!' *O God, grant the dreamers a harvest of justice and peace and joy; in Jesus' Name.*

COSTLY PERFUME: PART I
Mary took a pound of costly perfume (John 12:1-8; v. 3).
Extravagance always bothers us, more in the church than in our personal lives. How do we balance the desire to give glory to God with the command to attend to the needs of the poor? Jesus gives permission for effusive expressions of love for our Lord. In the end, it is not a question of one or the other. In Christ, we experience the extravagance of God's love for us, and we are authorized to give everything we have for the glory of God, whether it is helping the poor or making a generous offering. *Lord, Jesus, forgive me when I want to be a cheap disciple.*

COSTLY PERFUME: PART II
. . . a pound of costly perfume (John 12:1-8; v. 3).
A Roman pound was 12 ounces, which would be a good sized container of costly perfume. Mary apparently could afford it. Jesus our Savior and Lord always deserves the best we can give of "ourselves, our time and our possessions." When Jesus quoted the first part of Deuteronomy 15:11, "You will always have the poor with you," perhaps the disciples remembered the rest of the verse, "Open your hand to the poor and needy neighbor in your land." The poor also deserve the best we can do, for Jesus' sake. *Lord God, may we never tire of remembering the poor.*

COSTLY PERFUME: PART III
The house was filled with the fragrance of the perfume (John 12:1-8; v. 3).
Loving Jesus is expensive. For Mary, it was pricey imported perfume. For Paul the Apostle, it was giving up his own righteousness, in order to have the righteousness from God through

faith in Christ (Philippians 3:4b ff.). For us also loving Jesus will cost us something—time, convenience, the scorn of our friends, maybe even money. *"In every place the fragrance that comes from knowing Christ spreads through us in every place"* (2 Corinthians 2:14).

PREROGATIVES

Christ Jesus . . . emptied himself (Philippians 2:5-11; vv. 5, 7).
Some people we know are full of themselves. Jesus emptied himself. This is amazing in itself, and more so when we realize he emptied himself of divine prerogatives. What wouldn't we give to have more prerogatives of any kind! "Have this mind," the Apostle writes, the mind of Christ. This is the divine secret. The last will be first; die to live; self-emptying in order to be filled with the grace and glory of God revealed in Jesus Christ. *Dear God, when I ask for humility I feel proud. If you will give me 'the mind of Christ' it will take care of everything.*

CHRIST CRUCIFIED

We proclaim Christ crucified (1 Corinthians 1:18-31; v. 23).
We are fully aware of the problems connected with the cross of Christ. Rational minds will puzzle over the mechanics of atonement, and religious enthusiasts will seek to bypass it. Nevertheless the power of God to release us from bondage to sin and death comes through the cross. In our own lives, it is when we experience the cross in times of weakness, suffering and defeat that God's triumph takes hold of us. We will not let go of the cross. It is our way to life. *In the cross of Christ I glory . . . Lo, it glows with peace and joy.* – John Bowring, 1792-1872

SCHEMES

But I trust in you, O LORD (Psalm 31:9-16; v. 14).

All around they scheme and plot, *but I trust that*, whatever else happens, whatever people may say, whatever misfortunes come my way, the Lord God will make his face shine on me. God is my help, my deliverer, my strength. The sign and pledge is the cross of Jesus Christ, where the Son of God takes on himself the scorn and hatred of every kind of conspiracy in order to save and rescue. *But I trust in you, O Lord.*

STIRRING

He stirs up the people (Luke 23:1-5; v. 5).

Woe to those complacent ones who are not stirred up by Jesus! The gospel of our Lord Jesus Christ is always stirring things up. The powers and authorities, spiritual and worldly, are threatened by the rule of God breaking into lives that are satisfied with the way things are. The life, death and resurrection of Jesus mark the end of the rule of sin, death and evil over us. For those who thirst for righteousness in their own lives and in the world, the coming of Jesus into any life will always stir things up. *Once again, dear God, you have stirred me up, in Jesus' Name.*

SCORNED

The leaders scoffed at him (Luke 23:32-43; v. 35).

Our own words often convict us. Jesus was not only flogged and crucified, but he was also mocked and scorned—by the king, the soldiers, and a criminal. Even the religious leaders scorned the one they derisively called Messiah. The Son of God is willing to be mocked and ridiculed by the very ones he came to save. He was despised and rejected, yet chosen by God to gather the lowly as well as the haughty, the insiders and the marginalized, the righteous and the criminals, into his grace. *Jesus, remember me when you come into your kingdom* (v. 43).

OUR DYING HOUR

This man . . . asked for the body of Jesus (Luke 23:50-56; v. 52).
The God we worship and adore is the One who came among us as a mortal, willing to suffer all things with us, willing to give up his spirit and die, and willing to experience the tomb just as all mortals must. The One who was despised and rejected was claimed in death by the courageous and noble Joseph of Arimathea. In the same way, the Lord Jesus claims us in our dying hour and promises that resurrection and life, not the tomb and oblivion, will be God's final word and will for us. *Father, into your hands I commend my spirit* (v. 46).

EASTER

III. Easter

. . . singing with full voice,

> *"Worthy is the Lamb that was slaughtered*
> *to receive power and wealth and wisdom*
> *and might and honor*
> *and glory and blessing!"*

--Revelation 5:12

A ROLLING STONE

They found the stone rolled away (Luke 24:1-12; v. 2).

Rolling the stone away from the gate of death is one of the things we cannot do for ourselves. At the entrance of the tomb—once sealed in the name of the Empire, God's will is open for inspection. When we show up, prepared to fulfill the obligations of mourning, we find that God has prepared a victory over sin, death, and evil. The stone is rolled away: there is forgiveness and life in Jesus' name. It was more than we had imagined possible, and we could not have done it by ourselves. *Break open, O God, my sealed heart, to let the joy and peace of Jesus in.*

PEACE

The message . . . peace by Jesus Christ. He is Lord of all (Acts 10:34-43; v. 36).

They put him to death, but God raised him. The time for getting even, or exacting punishment, is past. Behold, it is Easter, and that means there can be peace on earth. There is forgiveness of sins through the name of Jesus Christ. Enemies can forgive each other.

The vitriolic atmosphere of anger and insults and past grievances has been cleansed and purified by the death and resurrection of Jesus. The message is peace by Jesus Christ, peace between foes and peace with God. *Your peace, O Lord, be with those I love and with those who do not love me; for Jesus' sake.*

PERPLEXITY
They were perplexed about this (Luke 24:1-12; v. 4).
This is the best news we have heard today. The resurrection of Jesus left the visitors to the cemetery perplexed. What God has in mind for us cannot be calculated according to human expectations, nor can it be outlined or planned on the basis of what we know. In the mystery of God's will and power, Christ was raised from the dead. In the life of the believer, perplexity gradually yields to praise, glory, and joy. *O God, you are greater than all our thoughts put together. To you alone the glory!*

REJECTED
The stone that the builders rejected . . . (Psalm 118:14-29; v. 22).
Jesus was the stone that was chosen last. They took a look and dismissed his project of the kingdom as hopelessly unrealistic. Though Jesus was rejected in the most demeaning way, nevertheless, the power of God was revealed in the weakness of the cross. Now Jesus is Lord of all. God stands with those who are excluded, shamed, weak and confused. Christ Jesus, the stone that was rejected, has chosen us to be living stones in God's new temple. *Dear God, you are to be praised for making stones alive!*

THE FIRST DAY
Early on the first day of the week . . . (Luke 24:1-12; v. 1).
In our rush to squeeze the weekend for all its worth, more and more activities are planned for Sunday. Even Christians do not always remember to properly prepare to rest on the first day of the week.

On account of the resurrection of Jesus, we have boldly moved the Sabbath from the end of the week to the beginning. Sunday is not the last day of the weekend, where some modern calendars place it, but the day of new beginnings. The Lord's Day proclaims righteousness and life and the promise of God's rule stretching before us during the coming days. *Lord Jesus, may I boldly rest in the joy of your new beginning.*

ONE MORE SURPRISE*

The resurrection of the dead has also come through a human being (1 Corinthians 15:19-26; v. 21).

Let us glory in this promise that is beyond human comprehension or verification: we believe in the resurrection of the body! Jesus, truly God and truly human, entered into our humanity and died, as we shall die. The heart stopped beating; the flesh turned cold. The grave was closed and sealed. But because Jesus is bound inseparably to us, we close our eyes in expectation of "just one more surprise."* *Hold before us, Lord God, the promise that is beyond human comprehension.*

---

*The phrase is from John Ylvisaker, *Borning Cry,* Second Edition, Volume 1. Waverly: New Generations Publishers. 2000. Song No. 1, *I Was there to Hear Your Borning Cry.*

THE LAST ENEMY

The last enemy to be destroyed is death (1 Corinthians 15:19-26; v. 26).

Enemies bring death into the world because of their constant desire to eliminate the adversary. The last enemy, however, is not a person at all, but the sinister threat to snuff the life out of God's creation. Death is the enemy, and the resurrection of Jesus is God's answer. God wants enemies to find peace in Christ so that all can live. The rule of Christ will culminate in death's final defeat. *Thanks be to*

God who gives us the victory through our Lord Jesus Christ (1 Corinthians 15:57).

FULLNESS OF LIFE

"I am the Alpha and the Omega" (Revelation 1:4-8; v. 8).

The A and the Z, the beginning and the end, the first and the last, the motivation and the goal. The daily humdrum of routine and the exhausting rushing around can fool us into thinking that life meanders on without form or purpose. On the contrary, all of life flows into Christ. Nothing, however ordinary, is without purpose. Jesus gathers everything together—some things to be forgiven and others to be blessed—and brings us to fullness of life in the presence of God. *Lord Jesus, you are my first thought when I awake, and my last before sleep.*

PEACE . . . PEACE: PART I

"Peace be with you" (John 20:19-23; vv. 19, 21).

Some people come into the room saying, "Pleased to meet you." Jesus comes saying, "Peace be with you." In the dullness of routine, in the vague undercurrent of anxiety that runs through our lives, or in the thoughts of past wrongs and injustices either committed or suffered by us, Jesus comes in the full power of the resurrection and says, "Peace be with you." *Lord Jesus, I am always a little startled when you come into my life.*

PEACE . . . PEACE: PART II

"Peace . . . peace . . . peace be with you" (John 20:19-23; vv. 19, 21).

Jesus does not tire of comforting his disciples however frightened, skeptical or uncomprehending they may be. Whether jittery in the face of possible ridicule for our convictions, or cowering behind closed doors of our little community, Jesus calms our fears and puts courage into our hearts to trust the message of the resurrection and to be agents of forgiveness in an unforgiving world. *Lord Jesus, help me to believe your resurrection with courage and joy.*

A GREAT NOISE

Praise him with clanging cymbals (Psalm 150; v. 5).

In the Great Assembly of God's people no one is urged to sing less loudly, or play an instrument less boldly. There is a place for every kind of gift to be offered in praise and thanksgiving to the One who creates, saves, and makes holy. The thrill of the trumpet, the grace of the harp, even the tuneless crashing of cymbals are all invited, and no one is discouraged from joining in. If you have breath, let loose with whatever sound you can make to give your witness. *Dear God, at Easter even the rocks cry out, for Jesus' sake.*

WOUNDED

"Do not doubt, but believe" (John 20:24-31; v. 27).

The wounds of Christ are still visible. You may see them in the life of your neighbor, or you may see them in your own life. We have been beaten down, dismayed; we have gone through illness and adversity; we have experienced the hard things and the disappointments of life; and behold! We live. This is only possible though Jesus Christ. The Wounded One says simply, "Do not doubt, but believe." *Bless, Lord Jesus, with healing, resurrection power, those whose wounds show and those whose wounds are hidden from view.*

FOR OUR SAKE

. . . these are written so that . . . through believing you may have life in his name (John 20:24-31; v. 31).

The purpose of these central events in the Christians' year is to give us life in the name of Jesus. The birth, the signs and teaching, the suffering, death and resurrection: it was all for us, for our sake! –so that, freed from the persistent oppressions of sin and death, God might make us righteous and alive. We call on the Name of the crucified and risen Jesus Christ, and Behold! There is life. *Lord Jesus, let there be Life!*

THE KINGDOM

"We must obey God rather than any human authority" (Acts 5:27-32; v. 29).

Jesus, the firstborn of the dead, is now the ruler of the kings of the earth (Revelation 1:5). The world divides itself into little kingdoms that often do not know how to get along with each other and sometimes even have a hard time organizing themselves internally for the common good. We work and pray for the well-being of the place where we are called to be (Jeremiah 29:7), but our only ultimate allegiance is to Jesus Christ. We live in an earthly kingdom, of course, but we belong to a wider Kingdom where God has called us to serve as priests. Priests bring the suffering of the world to God, and bring the grace of the Lord Jesus to a world still perplexed about sin and evil and death. *Jesus, Lord of lords and King of kings, Sovereign Ruler, crowned in majesty and splendor, may no other claim challenge my loyalty to you.*

Remember, if the grace of God hath taken hold of thy soul, thou art a person of another world, and indeed a subject of another and more noble kingdom, the kingdom of God.

--John Bunyan, 1628-1688

EMPTY NETS

"You have no fish, have you?" (John 2`:1-14; v. 5).

It could be the result of a day's effort. It could be the feeling we get when there is a cluster of bad news. Perhaps it is the strange realization that comes to us as we celebrate another birthday. Jesus is on the beach for that very reason. He knows where the emptiness is and he comes to fill it. *Lord Jesus, when I come up empty you send me back with a new idea.*

LOVE IS TESTED
"Do you love me more than these?" (John 21:15-19; v. 15).
Are you a super disciple, or an ordinary one? Do you love Jesus more than everyone else? We will not know unless our love is tested. Peter's love was tested in the courtyard of the high priest's house, and tested again on the beach. We have moments of faithfulness and moments when faith vanishes with our courage. Our gracious Lord Jesus Christ meets us on the beach and gives us another chance to say, *Yes, Lord, you know that I love you.*

GLORY
. . . myriads of myriads and thousands of thousands . . . (Revelation 5:11-14; v. 11).
The ineffable glory and splendor of God's Presence is usually visible only by faith. A few, precious few, like John of Patmos, have had visions; the rest of us can only imagine. While quotidian life rolls on with its ordinariness punctuate by moments of joy or sorrow, "the Lamb that was slaughtered" rules by grace and mercy, and is praised by the unseen hosts of heaven. Our faithful songs of praise enable us to stand with the myriads and myriads who give blessing and honor to the Lamb. *Glory to you, Lord Christ, forever and ever.*

A MOMENTARY STING
His anger is but for a moment; his favor is for a lifetime Psalm 30: v. 5).
We cry "Grace, grace!" but sometimes we forget why. There is grace because there is also sin. We claim the grace of God just exactly because we have also seen "God's righteous frown." We wander in and out of the paths of righteousness. The rod and staff may sting momentarily, but it gets us back to where we need to be, enjoying

God's favor throughout our lives and beyond. *Lord God, I thank you for being gracious to me, for Jesus Christ's sake.*

ALWAYS JESUS
Worthy is the Lamb (Revelation 5:11-14; v. 12).
We cannot praise Jesus too much. Jesus in the morning, Jesus in the evening, Jesus at noontime. The cross stands as witness that Jesus is our strength and help as we consider the monumental daily tasks that await us. Jesus is our resting place in the midst of the multi-tasking busyness of the day. Jesus is the welcome embrace to comfort when all is done or undone. Let the praise and blessing and glory mount up to honor Jesus Christ, who has won the battle for us. *To you, Lord Christ, blessing and glory and power and honor and . . . . !*

THE ART OF ARRIVING AT AMEN
It is not very easy.
There always seems to be something to add.
--Søren Kierkegaard (1813-1855)

GREAT CHANGE
"Lord, I have heard from many about this man . . ." (Acts 9:10-20; v. 13).
If God raised Jesus from the dead, why should we doubt that God can reverse and transform lives? Perhaps you have been praying for someone's life to undergo great change. Do not despair. At the right time God's power will be revealed. In the meantime, perhaps someone is praying for you! God's Spirit is at work to lift the scales from our eyes, too. *O God, let there be renewal, and let it begin with me.*

A LITTLE HELP

For several days he was with the disciples in Damascus (Acts 9:10-20; v. 19).

The fellowship of believers is really indispensable. Not even the brilliant Apostle Paul was able to figure things out for himself. We are indebted to those unnamed disciples in Damascus for having helped Paul. Led by the Spirit, they were patient with the one who had come to do them harm and ended up preaching the gospel he had formerly persecuted. None of us has a monopoly on Christian truth. The Spirit uses everyone's gifts to weave together our Christian witness. *I am grateful, dear God, for all my teachers in Christ.*

THE GOOD SHEPHERD: PART I

"My sheep hear my voice" (John 10:22-30; v. 27).

If a key to growth in the church is spiritual renewal, it will begin with careful, earnest, profound listening to the Shepherd's voice. The words of the Good Shepherd will not be effective if the Shepherd's words are left behind somewhere between the pews. The words of Jesus are intended to go with us, and grow with us, and color every personal relationship, every job situation, every use of our time and money. If we do not close our ears, the words of Jesus will echo and reverberate to challenge and comfort. *Lord Jesus, I will be quiet now and listen.*

THE GOOD SHEPHERD: PART II

"My sheep hear my voice" (John 10:22-30; v. 27).

Voices come at us from all directions. There is something interesting on the television. At the same time a family member has something important to tell us. And we can't keep our eyes off the mobile device glued to our hands. Then there are the voices within that urge us in one direction or another. Through it all, perhaps faintly in the background, is the voice of the Good Shepherd, patiently calling, never giving up, drawing us to his side, for life and joy in his Presence. *Dear God, in the many sounds of the day help me to discern your voice.*

A FINE EXAMPLE

There was a disciple . . . she was devoted to good works and acts of charity (Acts 9:36-43; v. 36).

If you are looking for a picture of the new life in Christ, you might look at this woman best known by her Greek name Dorcas. Scripture says we are ". . . created in Christ Jesus for good works" (Ephesians 2:10). "Good works and acts of charity" *is* our way of life in Christ. Dorcas has led the way, and we do well to follow her example. *Help us, Lord, to follow the example of Dorcas, who teaches the meaning of 'devotion.'*

PSALM 23

The LORD is my shepherd (Psalm 23; v. 1).

There are other shepherds, but not good ones. Our own interests and desires, and the desire to please other people pull and push us in different directions. If we do not know who our Shepherd is, we can easily be led to places where we do not want to go. In baptism the Lord Jesus Christ has claimed us and made us his own. It is Jesus who is our Shepherd, leading and guiding us in paths of righteousness, and helping us up when we stumble. *Dear Good Shepherd, lead me.*

ALL SEASONS

It was winter . . . (John 10:22-30; v. 22).

There is always a context for the shepherding of Jesus. The "darkest valley" sometimes lies before us in the winter of our lives, and even in the springtime as well. All the seasons and times of our lives provide the time and place where God's faithfulness to us through Jesus Christ becomes real. We cannot always count on the pleasure of basking in the mild air of a post-rain spring day. We can be sure that, when the cold winds of difficulty, sadness or anxiety send their chill, the voice of the Shepherd calls us to follow him and he will lead us safely through. *Lord Jesus, you are surely a Shepherd for all seasons!*

CALLED BACK
"No one will snatch them out of my hand" (John 10:22-30; v. 29).
Backsliding is harder than it looks. The devil, the world and our own flesh try hard, but Jesus will not let us go. There are times when neither flesh nor spirit are willing, but the Spirit of Jesus always calls us back. We sometimes wonder whether we will keep a steady witness in times of distress. Our faith wavers, it is true, but it is the Lord Jesus who keeps faith with us. *Faithful Shepherd, your love is stronger than my rebellion.*

WHO ARE THESE?
. . . the great ordeal (Revelation 7:9-17; v. 14).
Those who first read this strange Book of Revelation did not have to puzzle over whom the seer might be talking about. Christians, likely in the midst of persecution, found great comfort in these words. The comfort is for us as well: those whose conscience compels them to take a stand against the current; those who experience painful or debilitating illness and yet keep the faith; those who suffer heartache over a family situation; those who cry out in prayer and never seem to have an answer; and all the others who know the meaning of "ordeal." These are the ones whom God redeems by the blood of Christ. *Dear Jesus, by your resurrection power, comfort those passing through an ordeal on this day.*

JUST AS...

"Just as I have loved you . . ." (John 13:31-35; v. 34).

The cross of Jesus shows us that love is more than mere emotion. Love is preeminently sacrifice for the sake of the other. It is that way in marriage; it is that way between co-workers; it is that way in the church among believers. That is how God shows his love for the world (John 3:16). The love of Christ for us is both motive and model of Christian love. The cross also enables us to do what we could not have done on our own. *Give me courage, O God, to embrace the 'just as' clause.*

LIFE AFFIRMING

. . . the home of God is among mortals (Revelation 21:1-6; v. 3).

Many images and ideas of "the life to come" are really life-denying. Here is a word of hope that is life affirming: not an escape from this world but "a new heaven and a new earth." Once again the gospel reverses the direction of our thoughts. We are accustomed to the idea of "going to heaven." Here it is heaven that comes to us! God's home is among mortals. If this old earth is wonderful beyond description, imagine . . . the new earth! *Lord God, when you are in our home there is already a newness.*

THE LAST WORD

Death will be no more (Revelation 21:1-6; v. 4).

There comes a day when one suddenly realizes one is in the last half of one's life. Or maybe even the last third or quarter! God's answer to the question of death is the resurrection of Jesus. God's will and promise in the day of the new heaven and new earth is that "death will be no more." The last word always belongs to God, and God's last word is life through Jesus Christ our Lord. *Dear God, as the shadows lengthen, I am willing to let you have the last word.*

GLORIOUS SENTINELS

Praise him, sun and moon (Psalm 148; v. 2).

What a lonely place is the moon. Lonelier still our bright sun, that blazing, unapproachable furnace that means life for our planet. Sun, moon, and stars, lonely, glorious sentinels in the sky that keep everything spinning in order, they both inspire our praise of God and join in it. "If these are silent," Jesus said, referring to his followers, "the rocks will cry out." Sun, moon and stars give silent and wondrous praise to the Creating Love that brings all things into existence. *Looking at the stars, my silent awe is also praise, dear God.*

VIBRANT LEAVES

To the thirsty I will give water as a gift (Revelation 21:1-6; v. 6). Some are suddenly alone and crave companionship; some are victims of bad advice or bad company; some have betrayed their own values; some are simply the victims of unfortunate circumstances—they all come crawling and gasping into the Oasis that is Jesus Christ. It is Jesus who satisfies our deepest needs for love and forgiveness. Whether loneliness, guilt or despair, we are not lost to the heat. In Jesus, our wilted leaves gain strength and vibrancy returns. *You are Life to me, Lord Jesus.*

NO DISTINCTIONS

"The Spirit told me . . . not to make a distinction between them and us" (Acts 11:1-18; v. 12).

Making distinctions is just about the easiest thing to do. The new student, the new member, the foreigner—putting people in their place is so easy! For the early church there was one surprise after another: the resurrection, then the outpouring of the Holy Spirit, and then—even outsiders (Gentiles) come to faith in Christ, and suddenly, there are no distinctions at all. *Holy Spirit, train my mind for the distinction-less life in Christ.*

LEFT BEHIND

"God has given even to the Gentiles the repentance that leads to life" (Acts 11:1-18; v. 17).

When the good news of Jesus Christ infuses us with newness, there is something that is pushed out and left behind. Leaving something behind belongs to the dynamics of repentance. We are so tied to what we need to get rid of we could not do it without help. Even repentance is God's gift to us! The newness is a sign of God's grace, but the jettisoning of the old is also part of the dynamics of transformation. By grace, God gives us a repentant heart and spirit! *Dear God, direct my attention to the attitudes and behaviors I need to let go, with no regrets.*

CALLED

. . . convinced that God called us (Acts 16:9-15; v. 10).

One of the unique features of the Christian faith is the concept of "call." Churches are sometimes erroneously grouped with "volunteer organizations." We are not Christians because we volunteered. We are disciples because "the Holy Spirit has called us through the gospel . . ." (Luther's *Small Catechism,* explanation to the Third Article of the Apostles' Creed). We are under the call of Christ to be his disciples and our daily life's work (parent, child, student, spouse, worker) is also a calling, where God uses the gifts God himself has given us to bring the grace of the Lord Jesus into our world. *You have called me, Dear Jesus, to be a disciple. I am convinced of it.*

STEP BY STEP

". . . the Advocate . . . will teach you everything" (John 14:23-29; v. 15.

No one learns everything all at once. Part of being taught is learning to wait. The things at the back of the book look interesting, but we cannot make sense of them until we master the first chapter. We are all at one stage or another on the way to 'the full stature of Christ.' Christian maturity, Christian wisdom, is also a gift of the Spirit. Jesus promises that the Spirit, the Advocate, will teach us everything, step by step, day by day. To trust Jesus is to trust the guidance of his Spirit also. *Holy Spirit, I am a slow learner. Teach me only what is necessary for today.*

THE TREE OF LIFE
. . . the leaves of the tree are for the healing of the nations (Revelation 22:1-5; v. 2)

Health care is a basic human necessity. The seer of Patmos has a vision of the Tree of Life whose leaves bring healing to the nations. On That Day, the Day of our Lord Jesus Christ, perfect healing! It is interesting that the Book of Revelation, so weird in many respects, is at the same time down to earth. No floating along in puffy clouds strumming a harp in this vision. The New Jerusalem, City of God, has trees and fruit, and the Lamb! --face to face with his servants. *O God, we anxiously wait for the healing of your creation.*

WORLD AFFAIRS
You . . . guide the nations upon earth (Psalm 67; v. 4).

God's concern is not only for our daily bread, which by God's hand the earth graciously produces, but also extends to the affairs of the nations that occupy the face of this earth. In our view, the march of history is disorganized and chaotic. Our heartfelt trust is that, beneath the dust of human confusion, God is in control and will finally have the last, triumphant word that will guide the nations in the paths of righteousness and peace. *Sovereign Lord God, as we wait for the Day of our Lord Jesus Christ, bring order out of chaos among the nations of the world.*

ASCENSION DAY
They were continually in the temple blessing God (Luke 24:44-53; v. 53).

Waiting for "power from on high" they were drawn to the house of prayer. They could not stay away. Day by day they were rejoicing and speaking of God's great act in the death and resurrection of

Jesus. Worship, praise, prayer, fellowship—all originate in our acknowledgment that Jesus is the Ascended Lord, exalted above every authority and power, before whom all knees bend and to whom all owe obedience. Then the power from on high will teach us what we are to do. *Come, Power from on High, energize my feeble faith, in Jesus' Name.*

Today is Ascension Day, and that means that it is a day of great joy for all who can believe that Christ rules the world and our lives. –Dietrich Bonhoeffer (1906-1945), *Letters and Papers from Prison.*

NO TROUBLE

"Do not let your hearts be troubled . . ." (John 14:23-29; v. 27).
We will not be able to arrive at that place where we are neither troubled nor fearful unless we first acknowledge the things, circumstances, people, and trends that trouble us. These become our offering which we lay at the feet of Jesus. When we let go of these there is a momentary sinking feeling. We fear we are empty, powerless to struggle with the very things that trouble us, and of course we are. We empty ourselves in order to be filled with the peace of Jesus which we ourselves cannot give. *I believe that you rule the world, Lord Jesus. I pray for a trouble free heart.*

BEING ONE

". . . that they may be one . . . that the world may believe that you have sent me" (John 17:20-26; v. 21).
The oneness of Christians throughout the world has not always been our chief desire. If this is Jesus' prayer, it needs to be our prayer and desire as well. Embracing other Christians, in spite of our differences, becomes a witness and a means to the fulfillment of Christ's own prayer. The common witness of Christian people is for the sake of the world that God loves, so that the world may believe

that Jesus is God's means to fulfill our unmet needs and unknown desires. *Dear Jesus, give me a desire for oneness with my fellow believers, especially the ones I don't agree with.*

MAKING GOD KNOWN: PART I

"Righteous Father, the world does not know you" (John 17:20-26; v. 25).

This short statement of Jesus serves as a summary of the sad state of the world. Many think they know God, and say things about God, and pretend to speak for God. Many others have simply not made room for God in their lives. It is Jesus who has made God known to us. We will discover God's glory, love and purpose for the world when we give our full attention to Jesus. *It is through Christ, heavenly Father, that I make bold to stand in your Presence.*

MAKING GOD KNOWN: PART II

"Righteous Father, the world does not know you, but . . . these know . . ." John 17:20-26; v. 25).

We live in a time of keen interest in what is loosely called "spirituality." There are so many spiritual theories available that one can go through the line and pick a little of this, please, and none of that, thank you. Search, hunt, speculate—but still God the Father remains unknown. We point people to Jesus Christ because it is God's Son in the flesh who reveals God to us. *Holy Spirit, you have pointed me to Christ, who reveals the Father. May my witness always direct people to Christ.*

IDOLS

All worshipers of images are put to shame (Psalm 97; v. 7).

Our task is to discover where the images have been hidden. We get close to the idols when we feel our muscles tighten and our sense of humor leaves us. "In God we trust" is imprinted here and there, but one could ask if it isn't rather "a strong defense"; or a "favorable stock market"; or even a "winning season" that gives us reason to trust, relax, and find contentment. Against false comforts, the psalmist says, "the LORD guards the lives of his faithful." *Make me sensitive, Lord, to the places where the idols in my life are hidden.*

SINGING HYMNS

About midnight Paul and Silas were praying and singing hymns to God (Acts 16:25-34; v. 25).

They were securely fastened in the innermost cell and their feet bound as well, but nevertheless they were free. They could have felt sorry for themselves. They could have clenched their teeth and muttered something about "divine justice." They could have been angry with God, in whose service they found themselves in a painful situation. In the freedom of the gospel, in the power of the Spirit of Jesus, they prayed and sang. Blessing will find us in the oddest places. *When I feel trapped, put a song in my heart and on my lips, dear God.*

I AM

"I am . . . the bright and morning star" (Revelation 22:12-21; v. 16).

"I am . . . the Good Shepherd . . . the Way . . . the Truth . . ." and now, "the bright morning star." We probably don't spend enough time looking at the sky. We watch the clock; we watch television; we check the internet. Hovering over it all, the silent Sentinel announces the dawn of a new day. Jesus Christ, crucified, risen, exalted Lord of all, draws our attention beyond the mundane, the tragic, the sensational, to what is truly sublime—the majestic love of God that shines serenely in Jesus Christ to bring light to our darkness. *On this ordinary day, help me to see your glory, in the grace of Jesus Christ.*

AMEN

The grace of the Lord Jesus be with all the saints. Amen (Revelation 22:16-21; v. 21).

The last verse in the Bible is something we can hang on to. Whether life is stable or uncertain; whether we feel close to God or distant; whether our witness has been bold or timid—we can count on the grace of God in Jesus Christ. In fact, our mission and purpose in life is to draw more and more people into the grace of the Lord Jesus Christ. *Amen!*

PENTECOST

IV. Pentecost

About a hundred twenty, more or less,
Together, drawn by those who said they'd seen
Their Lord alive; they ask what could it mean?
Quite unaware the gift they would possess.
The promised Spirit came in midst of flames
Enabling witness; just as they'd been told.
The Power from on High had made them bold
To say the Name above all other names.
The talk then turns to gifts of Holy Ghost;
Afraid, not sure of what could be in store;
When Holiness is near, some close the door;
Yet who will stand against God's Pentecost?
No need dismiss exotic gifts so swift,
It's faith in Christ the Spirit's prim'ry gift.

FULLY ALIVE

When you send forth your spirit they are created (Psalm 104:25-37; v. 30).

The word for 'spirit' also means breath or wind. Without God's breath we are merely clods of clay. It is not by accident that we are inhabitants on this round piece of rock and dirt called Earth. When God's Spirit breathes into our nostrils we are fully awake and alive and aware that we are created by God and for God. We have the breath of life—God's Spirit—in our lungs and bones and tissue, to glory our Creator, Redeemer, and Comforter in all that we do. *Breathe on me, Breath of God.*

A BIG PROMISE

"If in my name you ask me for anything, I will do it" (John 14:8-17; v. 14).

Here is another promise that is so big and great that we are reluctant to take it to heart. When we ask for something "in the name" of Jesus, we will ask for whatever is consistent with the mission and purpose of Jesus. Since we hardly know what to ask for, *that* should be the subject of our prayers. *Lord, what do we need from you?*

FOR SLOW LEARNERS

"The Advocate, the Holy Spirit . . . will teach you everything" (John 14:25-27; v. 26).

What a comfort to know that we who are dull and slow to catch on will be taught what we need to know about Christ by the Holy Spirit. Questions and challenges to our faith arise almost daily. We are not left to wander aimlessly in a fog, searching for answers. The same Spirit of Jesus Christ, who was given at baptism and who led us to faith in Christ, will also teach us "everything." *Come, Holy Spirit, God and Lord / Be all thy gifts in plenty poured.* *

EVERY ONE OF THEM

All of them were filled with the Holy Spirit (Acts 2:1-21; v. 4).

We don't all speak in tongues but we are all filled with the Holy Spirit, and we all have gifts of the Spirit distributed among us for the well-being of the Body of Christ. The prophet Joel already saw it: "All flesh . . . sons . . . daughters . . . old men . . . both men and women . . ." (Joel 2:28). God has filled us, too, with the Spirit, to bring us to faith in Christ and to give honor and glory to his name. We should never doubt that we have, in abundance, the gifts that are needed for our Christian faith and life. *O, by the brightness of thy light / In holy faith all men unite / And to thy praise, by every tongue, / In every land, our hymn be sung. Alleluia! Alleluia!*

---

*Martin Luther, in *Service Book and Hymnal* (1958), No. 122; tr. Edward Traill Horn III.

UNINHIBITED JOY

"They are filled with new wine" (Acts 2:1-21; v. 13).

Sometimes people speak the truth without knowing it. Of course the believers were filled with new wine! Not the wine that comes from grapes, but the kind that comes from the power of the Holy Spirit to free and transform lives through Jesus Christ. Wherever God's Spirit passes to touch lives and bring them into contact with Jesus, there will be uninhibited joy and gladness. *Holy Spirit, fill me with the new wine of Christ.*

REMEMBER!

"The Spirit . . . will remind you" (John 14:25-27; v. 26).

Just when we are welling up with self-righteousness, the Spirit reminds us that "all have sinned" and stand in need of the grace of God. Just when we allow anger to overtake us, the Spirit reminds us that Jesus commanded us to love our enemies. Just when anxiety about money or another issue causes us to lose control, the Sprit reminds us to trust God for all our needs. We are forgetful, and we don't always remember the commandments Jesus gave us, but the Spirit is ever present to remind us! *Holy Spirit, remind me of the Way of Christ.*

CHILDREN OF THE HEAVENLY FATHER

Abba! Father! (Romans 8:14-17; v. 15).

The Spirit of Jesus, which is the Holy Spirit, teaches us that we are really and truly children of God and God is really and truly our Father. In the power of the Spirit we are led to recognize that our

Father in heaven is loving and not cruel; that God forgives for Jesus' sake and does not punish; and that God is not capricious, inflicting hardship here but not there. *Abba! Father! Padre! Vater! Far! Pai!* In whatever language the word means tenderness, compassion, and love, for time and eternity. *Father, hear me, for Jesus' sake.*

THE SPIRIT OF TRUTH: PART I

"I still have many things to say to you, but you cannot bear them now" (John 16:12-15; v. 12).

The Christian life is always a learning process. That is why it is called "discipleship." As disciples, learners, we follow our Master, discovering day by day what life in the world for Jesus' sake will be for us. Since discipleship means, above everything else, life in the cross, of course we cannot bear the "many things" now. Each day's challenge is sufficient for the day. So also the grace of our Lord Jesus is sufficient to make our faith consequential. *Lord Jesus, as a lifelong learner, what lesson will I learn today?*

THE SPIRIT OF TRUTH: PART II

The Spirit of truth . . . will guide you into all the truth (John 16:12-16; v. 13).

No one knows everything, and no one learns everything about Jesus all at once. We all grow in our faith in different ways, according to the working of the Spirit. This may provoke frustration or jealousy, but what is common to all who are led by the Holy Spirit is faith in Jesus Christ. Faith comes in and out of focus as we go through life, sometimes shining brighter, sometimes a little dimmer. The trustworthy promise of Jesus is that the Spirit will guide us into all the truth. *Holy Spirit, when I am lost in the fog, take my hand.*

THE SPIRIT OF TRUTH: PART III

The Spirit of truth . . . will glorify me (John 16:12-15; vv. 13-14).

We sometimes forget, easily distracted as we are by other priorities, that the purpose of our worship, our life as a congregation, and our lives as Christian people in the world is to glorify Christ. The Holy

Spirit points us to Christ, brings us to faith in Christ, and empowers us to live in such a way that Jesus is honored and glorified in our speech and action. *Glory to you, Lord Jesus Christ.*

DROOLING BABIES

Out of the mouths of babes and infants you have founded a bulwark because of your foes (Psalm 8; v. 2).

Our witness often comes out as though we were inarticulate babblers. God's power is revealed in signs of weakness, the cross of Christ being the chief example. Here we learn that even the babbling of drooling babies establishes the power and glory of God against which God's enemies will not prevail. Whatever is done in word or deed in response to God's grace in Jesus Christ stands as a mighty bulwark against sin, death and the power of evil. *Thine is the power, and the glory, forever.*

THE WISEST GENERATION

Does not wisdom call, and does not understanding raise her voice? (Proverbs 8:1-4; v. 1).

Surrounded by electronic gadgetry and mechanical wizardry of every kind, we imagine ourselves to be the wisest of any generation that ever walked on earth. Wars, human cruelty, inequalities and injustices, family disintegration and the scarcity of ordinary kindness all reveal the emptiness of that conceit. God's wisdom is Christ (I Corinthians 1:24), crucified to put evil away and to reconcile us to God and enemies to each other. *Holy Wisdom of God, deliver us from our foolishness.*

FEELING GOOD

. . . we also boast in our sufferings (Romans 5:1-5; v. 3).

What a difference there is between "feeling good" and boasting of one's sufferings! Suffering—whether it is the result of our Christian witness or simply because we are subject to ordinary circumstances surrounding human life—always leads us to Christ. The cross is where God's love is made real. In our eagerness to "feel good" it would be too bad if we wasted the experience of suffering by allowing anger or bitterness to push God's love away. *Dear God, when I am not feeling good, I look for love in the cross of Christ.*

A RUSHING TORRENT

God's love has been poured into our hearts through the Holy Spirit (Romans 5:1-5; v. 5).

The glass is neither half empty nor half full. It is filled to the brim, overflowing. My cup runneth over! The more we empty ourselves of the things that belong to Old Adam/Eve the more space we create for God's love. Here it comes, more and more, a rushing torrent of forgiveness to wash away the past and power for God to rule and direct your life. The past is forgiven, washed away. Behold, Christ, the love of God, lifts you and carries you along. *Surely, my cup runneth over!*

GRIEF: PART I

"What have you against me, O man of God" (I Kings 17:17-24; v. 18).

A child dies unexpectedly and we naturally look for answers. The distraught mother of the child in our reading thought it must have something to do with her. Perhaps she had sinned in some way that resulted in her son's death. God does not will misfortune or sadness for anyone. God's will for us is life, not death. In Jesus Christ God's will is the joy and gladness of a redeemed humanity and restored creation. This is prefigured in the words of the prophet, "See, your son is alive." *Dear God, help me to be patient while I wait for your deliverance.*

GRIEF: PART II

When the Lord saw her, he had compassion . . . (Luke 7:11-17; v. 13).

Jesus did not say, "God needed him;" or "God needed another angel." When Jesus saw the widow mourning the death of her only son, he had *compassion*. When God sees human sadness resulting from the death of a loved one, whether tender child or ancient patriarch, God has compassion. God's compassion is revealed in the Only Begotten Son, whose death and resurrection is the promise of our resurrection as well. In the face of death God's last word is life. *Heavenly Father, when I am struggling to find something comforting to say, at least help me to be compassionate.*

GRIEF: PART III

"Do not weep" (Luke 7:11-17; v. 13).

People who are grieving make us uncomfortable. Perhaps it is because grief reminds us of how precarious our own life and well-being are. People try to comfort the bereaved however they can, sometimes with words that are not helpful. Only Jesus, the Lord of Life, can say, "Do not weep." The rest of us, who in ourselves have no power over death, should let the bereaved weep until they have no more tears. After the tears, and in the silence, it is Jesus who says, "I am the resurrection and the life' (John 11:25). *Make me sensible, Lord Jesus, to be part of the silence.*

BLESSING

I said in my prosperity, 'I shall never be moved . . .' (Psalm 30; v. 6).

Those who trust in their good fortune will always be insecure. Prosperity and other sources of contentment are often confused with blessing. Blessing, however, is perceived most acutely when there is nothing else we can hang onto except God's grace. When false comforts let us down, we learn to trust. In times of economic uncertainty, or when we deal with the capriciousness of nature, or the deception of human institutions, what is solid is God's grace revealed in Jesus Christ. *I marvel, Lord God, at those who have nothing, but trust in you completely.*

TRANSFORMATION: PART I
You have heard of my earlier life . . . (Galatians 1:11-24; v. 13).
Some testimonies of a former life are filled with debauchery and degradation. Paul's former life was one of righteousness according to the law of God. The Lord Jesus came into Paul's life bringing a different kind of righteousness. God's own righteousness is not forced or compelled, but freely changes hearts and minds, attitudes and behaviors. Rigidity and judgment can also be changed into graciousness, patience and love for God and neighbor, for Jesus Christ's sake. *For Jesus' sake, dear God, do not remember . . . those things.*

TRANSFORMATION: PART II
God set me apart . . . called me to reveal his Son to me . . . (Galatians 1:11-24; v. 15).
We see God's intervention in our lives, first of all, in our sense of being called to faith in Jesus Christ. Then we are called, set apart, appointed, to serve our Lord Jesus Christ in some particular way according to the gifts, skills, and interests that God has given us. Even before we were born it was God's purpose to love us in Jesus Christ and use us as vehicles for that love for the world. *Father in heaven, I have heard your call.*

TRANSFORMATION: PART III
"The one who formerly was persecuting us is now proclaiming the faith he once tried to destroy" (Galatians 1:11-24; v. 23).
Can attitudes, whose roots go deep, formed since childhood and hardened by the tough knocks of life, be changed, renewed, and transformed? Those who knew Paul—before and after—could testify to what they had seen. If there was hope for Enemy Number

One of the Christian faith, there is hope that the attitudes and behaviors that we carry around can also be bent and shaped to conform to the image of Christ within us. *You are the potter, I am the clay.*

REFRESHMENT
Do not be like a horse or a mule (Psalm 32: v. 9).

Some people are so stubborn they would rather let their "strength dry up as by the heat of summer" than acknowledge their mistake. Why waste away when refreshment is available for the asking? "I said, I will confess . . . and you forgave!" The confession of sin always takes place in the context of God's grace through Jesus Christ. The result of forgiven transgression is happiness. *Gracious God, by your Spirit do not let stubbornness get in the way of my happiness.*

PLEASING GOD
The thing David had done displeased the Lord (2 Samuel 11:26-12:10; v. 27).

We know how to please ourselves, but we do not always know how to please the Lord. In fact, sometimes we even forget to ask the Question: How can I please God in this situation? We are justified by faith, and we have peace with God. For that very reason, so as not to disturb the peace, it is important to strive after the things that please God. Justice, holiness, purity, mercy, and service to our neighbor are some of the things that the peace of God brings to our minds. *How can I please you today, dear God?*

OUR STORY
"You are the man!" (2 Samuel 11:26-12:10; v. 7).

Stories about other people's misdeeds are interesting and sometimes appalling. What chills our soul is the realization that the story is ours. The Word of God is Law and Gospel. The Law says, "You are the one!" The Gospel of Jesus Christ not only announces forgiveness, but it gives us a new identity. In Christ, you are righteous! *More astonishing than my mistakes, O God, is your grace, through Christ.*

SOMEONE TO DEFEND THEM

A woman in the city who was a sinner . . . (Luke 7:36-8:3; v. 37).
To the one who gave the dinner and to all the guests, this woman must have been an unwelcome intruder. Yet her presence is what the Gospel is all about. Those who recognize they are "in bondage to sin" and cannot free themselves are just exactly the ones Jesus came to save. Those who come to Jesus weeping for their sins will always find forgiveness, and Someone to defend them against their accusers. *Just as I am, I come.*

A PROPHET

"If this man were a prophet, he would have known . . . (Luke 7:36-39; v. 39).
But he does know, and still he loves us. In fact Jesus knows us better than we know ourselves. We may admit to flaws in our character, tiny fractures, maybe, but the grace of the Lord Jesus is thorough-going cleansing and rebuilding. "Christ Jesus came into the world to save sinners" (1 Timothy 1:15). Jesus welcomes sinners and eats with them, not to condone sin, but to forgive us and free us from sin's power to condemn, corrupt and control. *Jesus, truly I am looking for you.*

MEASURING LOVE

"The one to whom little is forgiven, loves little" (Luke 7:36-50; v. 47).
If your love for Jesus Christ is measured in inches rather than yards or miles, it may be that you are a righteous person with little need for Christ at all. On the other hand, if things from the past (or

present) bother you, then acknowledge your sin and receive the full pardon and forgiveness of Jesus Christ. As you allow his grace to wash over you, let love for Jesus well up and overflow in a life of praise and service, in Jesus' Name. *Lord Jesus, I guess you have forgiven me more than I know; and I guess I love you more than I realize.*

A RIGHTEOUS PLACE
I do not nullify the grace of God (Galatians 2:15-21; v. 21).
Some feel they can make the world "a better place" by imposing their own scheme of morality on everyone else. The gospel makes the claim that God can make the world righteous by grace. The "law" does not make us righteous; it shows us our unrighteousness and our need for God. Paul puts it in stark terms. To glory in one's own goodness is to make Christ's death unnecessary. To throw oneself before God as though a "Gentile sinner" looking for mercy is to be clothed with the righteousness of Christ. *Father in heaven, I believe in the good news!*

CHRIST IN ME
It is Christ who lives in me (Galatians 2:15-21; v. 20)
There is comfort in 'wiping the slate clean,' but something deeper also happens when we are caught up in God's grace. "Crucified with Christ, it is no longer I who live, but Christ." No longer alienated from God, Christ lives in us. Not only do we walk in the presence of Christ, but Christ is present to the world through us. *O God, in Christ I am nearer to you than I ever thought possible.*

RESTRAINED
We were imprisoned . . . under the law . . . (Galatians 3:23-29; v. 23).
People who are a danger to society need to be put away so that they do not hurt anyone. Sad to say, people who come out of prison are not necessarily "corrected" by the experience. All of us need to be

restrained by the law because our natural inclinations are self-serving, rather than God- or neighbor-serving. The law restrains, but it does not change us. The grace of the Lord Jesus, received by faith, changes everything. *Lord God, I desire change in my inward being.*

SNEAKY

The law was our disciplinarian until Christ came . . . (Galatians 3:23-29; v. 24).

The law is for people who have no faith. "Before faith came," writes the Apostle, "the law was our disciplinarian." Then Christ came, the fulfillment and end of the law, and the beginning of righteousness. The strict disciplinarian made us sneaky. Chafing under the imposition of requirements, we looked for loopholes. Told "Do not" we desired to do the very thing prohibited. Now, by faith, we claim righteousness in Jesus' name. The Spirit is not a disciplinarian, but a Comforter, Advocate, and Guide, who gives us the desire to please God and shows us how to do it. *Give me new desires, Lord.*

CHRIST OUR GARMENT: PART I

You who were baptized . . . have clothed yourselves with Christ (Galatians 3:23-29; v. 27).

Baptized as babies or as adults, there is a helplessness we cannot overcome. We need the washing, the dying, the rising, the newness of it. The old will not do, but we are incapable of producing the new. The newness is Christ, his righteousness, his resurrection, his power to defeat sin and death. Christ is our garment, revealing our true nature, so that it is Christ Jesus who challenges the approach of every temptation, accusation or despair that comes our way. *Gracious God, let me never be content with the old, but always desiring the new, in Jesus' Name.*

CHRIST OUR GARMENT: PART II

You . . . have clothed yourselves with Christ (Galatians 3:23-29; v. 27).

Such a small thing, so great a gift. A few moments, a little water, a few words, but open the gift and behold! We are dressed in new clothes. Christ himself gives us a new identity and a new reality. The drama of Christ's life, death and resurrection plays out in our lives, every day, as we remember that we were baptized ". . . in the Name of the Father and of the +Son and of the Holy Spirit." *Triune God, I claim the baptismal gift.*

AN ANCIENT MEMORY

All the ends of the earth shall remember and turn to the LORD (Psalm 22:18-27; v. 27).

This psalm begins in utter abandonment but ends in a groundswell of praise, worship and adoration. The ancient memory of God's absolute claim and rule, embedded in the human soul, will come to light, and the "families of the nations" and even those "who sleep in the earth" will worship God, and not themselves, and "all nations" will acknowledge the dominion that belongs to God alone. This is the hope that springs from the cry of Jesus, "My God, why?" *Lord God, when I feel the weight of the cross, remind me of the resurrection.*

For the first time I examined myself with a seriously practical purpose. And there I found what appalled me: a zoo of lusts, a bedlam of ambitions, a nursery of fears, a harem of fondled hatreds. My name is Legion. —C.S. Lewis (1898-1963)

NAMING THE DEMONS

"What is your name?" He said, "Legion"; for many demons had entered him. (Luke 8:26-33; v. 30).

If only we had a single flaw—then maybe we could heal ourselves. There is too much wrong with us, however. We are beyond self-

83

help. Jesus comes to cleanse us of all unrighteousness. At his word we are freed, forgiven, healed of our iniquity. The sickness unto death scurries off, and we stand, trembling and a little shaken, but pure, righteous, and innocent before the Lord Jesus Christ. *Say the word, Lord Jesus, and I will be free.*

HOLINESS

The Gerasenes asked Jesus to leave them (Luke 8:32-39; v. 37). Perhaps the Gerasenes were afraid of the Presence of Holiness in Jesus. Our generation is not much impressed with holiness. In our day we look for scientific explanations—even for a herd of swine plunging over the cliff to their deaths. If we suddenly experienced a freedom from animosity, bitterness, jealousy, lust, greed, fearfulness, suspicion, we would not look to science for an explanation. The explanation is that the Holy One of God has approached to rescue us from the power of sin and transform us according to His Own Righteousness. *Dear Jesus, do not let me go over the cliff.*

VOCATION

"Return to your home" (Luke 8:34-39; v. 39).
Jesus says, "Go on home!" Very few Christians have the vocation of going far away to preach the gospel. The overwhelming majority, however, have the vocation (the 'call') to give witness to what God has done in their lives just exactly where they live and work today. At the stove, in your cubicle, with your tools, kissing your child goodnight, listening to your friend—this is where Christian faith is lived and practiced. *I am going home, Lord Jesus, with joy.*

THE NATIVITY OF SAINT JOHN THE BAPTIST
JUNE 24

. . . the messenger . . . is coming . . . and who can stand when he appears? (Malachi 3:1-4; vv. 1, 2).
When God sends a messenger to prepare the way, we should not be surprised if it causes us discomfort. We long for "the day of the

Lord" because the world needs to be made right, and we also need to be renewed and transformed. The messenger will draw our attention to sinfulness wherever it is found, and at the same time point the way to the Redeemer. In Christ, we are finally able to stand. *When your messenger is finished with me, stand me up, O God, in Jesus' Name.*

To another, he said, "Follow me": Part I
"Let the dead bury their own dead" (Luke 9:57-62; v. 60).
The call of Jesus trumps every other claim on our time and energy. When Jesus says, "Follow me," all other loyalties and allegiances become secondary. Most importantly the call of Jesus leads us out of ourselves, out of whatever little world we inhabit, so that Christ can make our burdens his own and so that we make the burdens of others our own. It is a life where there is no place to lay one's head except in the grace of the Lord Jesus Christ. *I have run out of excuses. I will follow.*

Follow me: Part II
. . . the fruit of the Spirit is love, joy, peace, patience, kindness, generosity, faithfulness, gentleness, an self-control (Galatians 5:13-25; vv. 22, 23).
If you 'follow' with wandering eye you may lose your way. The fruit of the Spirit will not mature in us if we are inattentive in the matter of following Christ. The gentle leading of the Holy Spirit focuses our attention on Christ, and to our surprise, we find ourselves in the midst of love, joy, peace, patience, and other wonderful godly characteristics. *Increase my attention span, Lord.*

Follow me: Part III
The boundary lines have fallen for me in pleasant places (Psalm 16; v. 6).
There is no freedom and no joy in aimlessness. We are most miserable when we don't know where we are going. In Christ, there

are boundaries to protect us from falling back into old patterns of behavior, and boundaries to define where our service and witness are to be carried out. The Lord has set us down in our place and in our unique circumstances. This is where the New Creation will be born and flourish in us. *I look around; I guess I am happy here and now.*

FOLLOW ME: PART IV
. . . those who belong to Christ have crucified the flesh (Galatians 5:16-25; v. 24).
We do not shape the new life that God gives us in our baptism. That would be a work of the flesh, the desire to have all things our way. To be a Christian is to die, and to experience the absolute helplessness of the tomb. In the mysterious power of God's Spirit, the earth quakes, the guards tremble, and we find that God has given us the victory in Jesus Christ over the old attitudes, thoughts and behaviors. "Behold, I make all things new" (Revelation 21:5). *Shake me up, Lord, for the total newness.*

FOLLOW ME: PART V
. . . you were called to freedom . . . (Galatians 5:13-15; v. 13).
We are called to freedom, but the paradox is that no one is fancy free. Even the far flung stars and planets are grasped by complex gravitational relationships. The question is, from what have we been freed, and to whom will we now be connected? The freedom we are called to is freedom from sin, death and evil by being bound to the Lord Jesus Christ. Freedom *from* sin is not freedom *to* sin. That would be slavery once again, and worse than before. The gospel tells us we have left the orbit of sin and have been grasped by the pull of God in Jesus Christ. *I give thanks to you, dear God, for gravity.*

FOLLOW ME: PART VI

. . . through love become slaves to one another (Galatians 5:13-25; v. 13).

Self-centeredness, laziness and an unwilling spirit are the biggest obstacles to the idea of loving our neighbor as ourselves. Christ gives us freedom from needing to be first and best. We are free to serve each other as slaves. Even if we are last, we are not left out. It sounds radical and it is. *Show me the peace and joy of radical love.*

FOLLOW ME: PART VII

"No one who puts a hand to the plow and looks back is fit for the kingdom of God" (Luke 9:57-62; v. 62).

The past has an ungodly attraction for us. Jesus calls us to discipleship. In gratitude and joy we grasp the plow's handle and move forward. But it is not quite what we expected. Old habits, old behaviors beckon. We forget how miserable we were. We forget the call of Jesus to be transformed under the yoke of his discipleship. Not fit for the kingdom? There are no harsher words than these. We are urged on by the promise, "My yoke is easy." *Only yoked to you, Lord Jesus, will the furrow be straight.*

SAINT MARY MAGDALENE
JULY 22

Mary Magdalene went and announced to the disciples, "I have seen the Lord" (John 20:11-18; v. 18).

There is a mystery about our new life in Christ, just exactly because it has to do with resurrection, which is totally outside of the human experience. We expect that people will always be selfish and rude, controlled by unhealthy desires, and condemned to be adversaries. When we see the stone has been rolled away, we can only wonder. Jesus is nearby to tell us what resurrection means. *By Word or Sacrament or any other Means, grant that we, with Mary Magdalene, may say, "I have seen the Lord!"*

A SILENT WITNESS

Bear one another's burdens, and in this way you will fulfill the law of Christ (Galatians 6:1-6; v. 2).

The five year-old boy was in the hospital with polio in the days before medical insurance was common. The bills were mounting. A Christian friend had earned some interest on a small investment. He gave the money to the boy's parents with a note that said simply, "Galatians 6:2." The note, a silent witness, was discovered many years later in the bottom of a drawer. *Praise to you, O God, for your faithful people.*

SEEDS FOR GROWTH

. . . if you sow to the Spirit . . . (Galatians 6:7-10; v. 8).

Paul the tentmaker takes us into the language of agriculture. He has spoken of the fruits of the Spirit—love, joy, peace, patience, etc. (Galatians 5:22f.). These are contrasted with the seeds that corrupt individual lives as well as the quality of life in community—enmities, strife, jealousy, quarrels, etc. (5:19f.). Those who sow peace and patience in the midst of jealousy and quarreling are often tempted to give up. The Apostle encourages us to "not give up," with the promise of a bountiful harvest. *Spirit of God, do not let me grow weary in doing right.*

CULTURE AND ROOTS

. . . the world has been crucified to me, and I to the world (Galatians 6:7-16; v. 14).

The "world" clings more closely to us than we probably imagine. We have ties to culture and our roots are deeply sunk into the soil of one place or another. Life in this world is marked by fierce rivalries, one piece of soil against another, each making its boast of nation or race or class. The cross of Jesus Christ free us from our mutual jealousies and mutual distrust. The place where we take our stand, the thing we boast of, is the cross of Jesus Christ. *Spirit of God, help me to recognize where the 'world' has me in its grip.*

THE JOY OF CREATION

All the earth worships you; they sing praises to you (Psalm 66; v. 4).
With senses keenly in tune with the grace and mercy of God, *all the earth* exults in waves and waves of gratitude and joy for the life God has given not just to us but to the whole creation. When our vision is limited to ourselves and to our way of life, we end up creating barriers and divisions between "them and us," and we miss out on the joy of God's creation. When we make God, rather than ourselves, the focus of our contemplation, we are caught up with *all the earth* in the joy of the Lord. *Spirit of God, catch me up, too, in the joy of your universe.*

THE HARVEST

". . . ask the Lord of the harvest to send out laborers into his harvest" (Luke 10:1-12; v. 2).
When there is an oil spill in the Gulf, ideas abound on how to clean it up. Not every idea is technologically feasible or appropriate. When the Church recognizes a vast spillage of souls, we anxiously feel the need to "Do something!" and do it real fast. Not every idea for 'church growth' is sound or feasible, or even Spirit generated. Against our anxiety, Jesus simply teaches us to pray for God to send laborers into the harvest. *Dear God, please send laborers into your harvest, for Jesus' sake.*

THE KINGDOM OF GOD

". . . say to them, 'The kingdom of God has come near to you'" (Luke 10:1-12; v. 9).
"Cure the sick," Jesus says, to our astonishment. Of course, *we* don't cure anybody. It is the power of the Name of the Lord Jesus Christ that works wonders in our midst. "Say to those you minister to, 'The

89

kingdom of God has come near to you'"—not because of us, but because of Christ in us. It is God's will that Christ Jesus should dwell in us, through faith and in the power of the Holy Spirit. If Jesus Christ wants his power made known through us, why should we resist it? *Thy kingdom come, Lord, and let the Name of Jesus Christ empower us.*

TASTY

The word is very near to you (Deuteronomy 30:8-14; v. 14).
Some people know how to taste their food. They can tell you if there is cumin or dill or whatever in the dish set before them. Others simply gobble it down without paying attention. The Word of God is on our lips and in our heart, available to be tasted in its exquisite simplicity. God's Word calls us into the abundant life of Jesus Christ. Some will taste it, and marvel. *Remind me, Lord, to savor your Word before putting it away.*

FAITH AND WORKS

. . . as you bear fruit in every good work (Colossians 1:1-14; v. 10).
Important things are often found in pairs: law and gospel; sinner and saint; faith and works. Faith and works are not enemies, but Christian characteristics that go hand in hand. Faith reveals itself in works of love, and the works point back to their origin in faith. As we "grow in the knowledge of God" we move into a deeper and clearer understanding of our participation in God's mission of loving the world and the people in it. *Spirit of God, awaken my faith to good works, for Jesus' sake.*

ON BUSINESS

. . . a Samaritan, while traveling . . . (Luke 10:25-37; v. 33).
The nasty stretch of road between Jerusalem and Jericho is apparently well traveled. People are going and coming, on holy business (priest and Levite), or on 'business' business (or whatever

the Samaritan's business was), or unholy business (thieves and brigands). In our day, our highways are filled with automobiles and trucks, racing back and forth. We seem to be always on the move, going someplace to do something. Now as then, at the edges of the busy-ness of modern life there are neighbors who need our attention. *With love for you and neighbor, make all my business a holy business.*

MANY PATHS

All of the paths of the LORD are steadfast love . . . (Psalm 25:1-10; v. 10).
Our earthly pilgrimage is not one straight line, but a succession of paths that bend this way and that, breaking off unexpectedly in new directions. Each path presents a degree of difficulty or arduousness that may please or distress us. Through it all we count on the steadfast love of the Lord. As we go, "He leads me in right paths," upheld by the steadfast love of God revealed in Jesus Christ. *Lord, when the direction of my life changes, it is a comfort to know you are there at the crossroads.*

PATIENT ENDURANCE

. . . be prepared to endure everything with patience . . . (Colossians 1:1-14; v. 11).
We admire the Good Samaritan's compassion; we should also take note of his patience. His compassion interrupted and delayed his journey. The requirements of spouse or child, crisis or illness, involve time, and the longer it takes the more anxious we become. As we become more Christ-like, we also become more patient. Or is it the other way around? *I am sure there is joy in patient endurance. Help me to find it.*

SELF-JUSTIFICATION: PART I

. . . wanting to justify himself, he asked Jesus, "And who is my neighbor?" (Luke 10:25-37; v. 29).

The lawyer makes a fatal, rookie mistake—asking a question for which he does not already know the answer! The answer Jesus gives will surprise him, and give him a standard to which he will never measure up. So we turn in faith to Christ for our righteousness, and being made righteous by faith, we can then in perfect freedom ask, *Show me how I can serve my neighbor.*

SELF-JUSTIFICATION: PART II

. . . wanting to justify himself . . . (Luke 10:29-37; v. 29).

When we have done all, there is still the nagging feeling that we have *not* done all. So we make comparisons and excuses and then we are in real trouble, because even adding everything up, it comes to very little. If Christ is our righteousness then everything has already been done. We are free to be Christ to our neighbor, free to lose ourselves in love and service. If righteousness depends on us, "the good" we do for our neighbor is really for ourselves. Let Christ be our justification, so that the righteous demands of the law may be carried out by Christ who dwells in us. *You have done all, Lord Jesus. I pray for a faith that loves.*

MARY AND MARTHA: PART I

Martha welcomed him into her home (Luke 10:38-42; v. 38).

"Listen! I am standing at the door, knocking . . ." (Revelation 3:20). It is not a middle school student raising money for a band trip. It is Jesus Christ who desires to be a permanent guest in your home and your life. The Presence of Jesus may be intimidating, but He comes to us for fellowship at the table, ours and His. If they said nothing else at your funeral except, "She (or He) welcomed Jesus," they would have said enough. *Come into my heart, Lord Jesus.*

MARY AND MARTHA: PART II

Mary . . . sat and listened (Luke 10:38-42; v. 39).

We do not have Jesus sitting right in front of us, so hospitality is not the issue. The issue is whether we are listening to Jesus. "Jesus unfiltered" is always a riveting experience. Sometimes we think we know what Jesus said, but then we read the words again and are astonished. The words of Jesus in the New Testament leap off the page to challenge and comfort. Like Mary, the more we listen the more we want. *Help me to be attentive, Lord.*

MARY AND MARTHA: PART III

She had a sister . . . who listened . . . (Luke 10:38-42; v. 39).

Our sympathies may be with one sister or the other, depending on our own inclinations. Some would rather just sit and talk; others need to be always doing something. We bring to light our own preference for reflection (Mary) or action (Martha) when we praise one or reprove the other. If we think Martha is too busy, perhaps it means we should get up and be a little busier ourselves. If we think Mary is too deeply involved in the mere words of Jesus, perhaps we should slow down and let Jesus' words fall on our ears and hearts as well. *Lord Jesus, lead me to the right balance of reflection and action in my life.*

QUALIFIED

O LORD, who may abide in your tent? (Psalm 15; v. 1).

The list of qualifications is a little bit disheartening. Who can say they "walk blamelessly and do what is right and speak the truth from their heart?" We need help from the Apostle who points us to Christ. "He has now reconciled [you] in his fleshly body so as to present you holy and blameless . . ." (Colossians 1:22). On the basis of Christ and his righteousness we claim a place in God's tent on the holy hill. *Gracious God, for Jesus' sake I dare enter.*

ABRAHAM: PART I

The Lord appeared . . . in the heat of the day (Genesis 18:1-10; v. 1).
Old Abraham was resting at the time of day when it is too hot to do
anything anyway. One wonders how God expects people to live in
such a climate. Suddenly, without warning, God is there. In the haze
of noonday heat, or perhaps in the questioning or grumbling about
the circumstances of our life, without warning God comes to bring
hope and restore us to meaning and purpose and mission. *Lord, when
you are near, it is never too hot nor too cold.*

ABRAHAM: PART II

Abraham ran . . . to meet them (Genesis 18:1-10; v. 2).
Strangers bring forth all of Old Abraham's energy. He runs, he
hastens, he urges and inspires other to alacrity. "I was a stranger,
and you welcomed me" (Matthew 25:35). The Lord God works his
way into our lives not only at the scheduled times of worship, but
also at unscheduled and inconvenient times. Jesus comes to us in the
lives of the stranger, the naked, the hungry. Discipleship means we
are going to be inconvenienced, maybe even daily, for the glory of
the name of Jesus Christ. *I pray for the energy of Abraham.*

A GOOD MYSTERY

. . . this mystery, which is Christ in you, the hope of glory (Colossians
1:15-28; v. 27).
There are things that need to be believed rather than analyzed,
especially mysteries. We can believe that Christ Jesus is the exalted
Lord of all. It might be harder to believe that the exalted Lord of all
is "in us." The two are really the same, because we are part of the
"all." Where there is faith in Christ there is also the indwelling Spirit
who brings us fullness of life with God, unhindered by sin or death.
When Christ is in us there is power over temptation, and there is
blessing for us and our neighbor that cannot be otherwise explained.
Keep me focused on this mystery.

V. Still Pentecost

It is truly meet, right and salutary,
that we should at all times, and in all places,
give thanks unto thee, O Lord, Holy Father,
Almighty, Everlasting God:
Therefore with Angels and Archangels,
and with all the company of heaven,
we laud and magnify thy glorious Name;
evermore praising thee, and saying:
Holy, holy, holy, Lord God of Sabaoth;
Heaven and earth are full of thy glory;
Hosanna in the highest.
Blessed is He that cometh in the Name of the Lord;
Hosanna in the highest.

THE LORD'S PRAYER: PART I
Your kingdom come (Luke 11:1-13; v. 2).
God's kingdom is not a place, but a rule. God's kingdom is wherever God rules. "God's kingdom comes on its own without our prayer, but we ask in this prayer that it may also come to us," Martin Luther says.* This is a dangerous petition, because it challenges the greed, self-centeredness, anger, anxiety, crazy desires and whatever else already rules in our hearts and lives. Asking God to rule in the world is to ask God to rule in us as well. Farewell, Old Adam/Eve.

Welcome, new creation in Christ! *Our Father in heaven . . . Your kingdom come!*

THE LORD'S PRAYER: PART II

Give us each day our daily bread (Luke 11:1-13; v. 3)
Jesus is not worried about having to live "from paycheck to paycheck" because he never had a paycheck anyway. Jesus lives day to day, and teaches us to do the same. "Do not worry about tomorrow. Let the day's own trouble be sufficient for the day" (Matthew 6:34). The sign of God's graciousness is that "God gives daily bread without our prayer, even to all evil people,"* says Martin Luther. To pray for today's bread is to free us from our anxiety and greed, and to acknowledge and give thanks for God's goodness. *Give us today our daily bread.*

---

*Quotes are from *Luther's Small Catechism,* © 1966 Augsburg Fortress.

THE LORD'S PRAYER: PART III

And forgive us our sins, for we ourselves forgive everyone indebted to us (Luke 11:1-13; v. 4).
"Everyone indebted to us" covers a lot of ground. Forgiveness is for all, not only for family and close friends and people we like, but also for enemies and those who hate us. To live by grace is not only to bask in God's forgiveness for us but also to embody the graciousness of God toward others. *Father, forgive them* is Jesus's prayer, and ours as well.

GOD AND THE GODS: PART I

. . . before the gods I sing your praise (Psalm 138; v. 1).
We put our lives on the line when we sing the praises of the God revealed in Jesus Christ, for thus we renounce any claim the "gods" might have on us. It requires as much courage as is humanly possible, and even more, because the gods of nationalism, tribalism,

capitalism, consumerism, way of life or life style and their devotees will pressure and scorn us if we do not bow down to the same idols. That is why, perspiring huge drops of sweat, we pray, *Save us from the time of trial.*

GOD AND THE GODS: PART II
I bow down toward your holy temple (Psalm 138; v. 2).
It is not the temple we worship, of course, but the God who meets us in the temple in word, water, bread and wine. We bow toward the holy temple to acknowledge that, even though God is everywhere present, we could not find him by ourselves, except where the Infinite is contained in the finite. In the noisy and busy world God may be silent. In the holy temple, where we arc silent, God speaks. *Our Father in heaven, hallowed be your Name.*

"The first duty of every soul is to find not its freedom, but its master. . . . If within us we find nothing over us, we succumb to what is around us . . . —P.T. Forsyth, 1848-1921

NEVER ENOUGH
"Be on your guard against all kinds of greed" (Luke 12:13-21; v. 15).
There is, of course, the insatiable thirst for money. There is never enough! Then there are the things money can buy—cars, property, electronic gadgets. Then there are things we want for free, or at the lowest possible cost, even if it means exploitation of those providing the service or product. The best antidote to greed is generosity. It is how God deals with us, ". . . who did not withhold his Own Son . . ." *Give us this day our daily bread.*

NO FUTURE
"I have no place to store my crops" (Luke 12:13-21; v. 17).
The one whom God called 'Fool!' in the parable did not stop to consider all his options. He had a bumper crop. Wise in his own

eyes, he thought God had given it all to him. If the barns that the rich man had were adequate in the past, they would have been adequate in the future as well—if only he had a future! The grace of the Lord Jesus teaches us that 'giving it away' is the Road to Riches toward God. *Even though I may be foolish, I pray that I may not be 'the Fool'.*

THE ULTIMATE POVERTY

"So it is with those who store up treasures for themselves" (Luke 13-21; v. 21).

Sooner or later everything we have will belong to someone else. We can either spend it or give it away, and if we spend it we will still have more that we cannot keep. Such is the ultimate poverty of those who store up treasures for themselves. A good housecleaning, it turns out, is good for the soul. When we locate our generosity gene, we find ourselves in synchronicity with God who is generous to us in every way. *Activate that generosity gene in me, Lord, for Jesus' sake.*

RANSOMED

Truly no ransom avails for one's life (Psalm 49:1-12; v. 7).

Jesus says that even if we worry about it we are incapable of extending our life even an hour (Matthew 6:27). We who live within the framework of birth and death know how precious our lives are. Rich or poor, clever or foolish, all are equally bound. Can we fool *Sheol* and live on forever? In Jesus Christ that is our claim. The ransom that avails is the death and resurrection of Jesus, by which God declares the invaluable nature of every human being. *I do worry about my span of life. Nevertheless, I believe that my life is in your hands.*

LOOKING UP

Set your minds on things that are above (Colossians 3:1-11; v. 2).

We who are caught up in this rough and tumble world of greed and deals and power and competition may find it hard to turn our gaze upward, not toward clouds and haloes and harps, but beyond, to the Ineffable Presence of God where righteousness, justice, purity, peace and mercy shine warmly and gloriously, where there is no hint of sin at all. How could we, sinful beings, think on these things, except through the grace of Jesus Christ? *Help me think on you, Lord God, in all your glory.*

PRACTICAL CHRISTIANITY

. . . seeing that you have stripped off the old self with its practices (Colossians 3:1-11; v. 9).

"Putting on Christ" is practical Christianity. When God makes us righteous in Christ there is a change that takes place, a change of clothes. Old practices—habits, behavior, attitudes—are discarded and replaced with different attitudes and behavior. Instead of a harsh word, we try on kindness. Instead of greed, we try on generosity. The new garment is Christ, who makes it possible to experience drastic changes. *Show me, gracious God, which new garment I should try on first.*

ALL NIGHT

. . . even at night their minds do not rest (Ecclesiastes 2:18-23; v. 23).

One works with skill and knowledge and someone else gets the benefit. How unfair! And staying awake at night worrying about it changes nothing! That is why, at the end of the day, we commit everything to the grace of the Lord Jesus: sins to be forgiven and work to be blessed. Then there is nothing left but to "go to sleep quickly and cheerfully" (Luther's *Small Catechism*). *I lie down and sleep; I wake again, for the LORD sustains me* (Psalm 3:5).

MARY, MOTHER OF OUR LORD
AUGUST 15

. . . all generations will call me blessed (Luke 1:46-55; v. 48).

August 15 has been observed since early times as the day of Mary's "falling asleep," that is, her death. Mary is "blessed" because through her God became a human being and delivered us from sin and death. It is the desire of Jesus to be incarnated in us, too. "Abide in me and I in you." To this end we may follow the example of blessed Mary. When told that she would be the mother of the Savior, she said, *"Here am I, the servant of the Lord."*

COUNTING STARS

Look toward the heaven and count the stars (Genesis 15:1-6; v. 5).

Other than adding a string of zeros at the end, we are really no closer to being able to count the stars than Abraham was, and perhaps God seems as distant to us as the stars. In the intensity of daily activities—feelings hurt, promises not kept, things we regret doing or saying—God's promised kingdom can seem far off. Christ, in the fullness of his grace, has promised to be among us in Word and Sacrament. *Gracious God, let me be satisfied to know you are present, whether I feel it or not.*

NOT SEEING

Faith is . . . the conviction of things not seen (Hebrews 11:1-3; v. 1).

The "not seen" is the hardest part of faith. We "believe" in the forgiveness of sin, but it still nags at us. We "believe" in the one holy, catholic and apostolic church, but we do not always see it. We "believe" in the resurrection of the body, but it seems easier to talk about disembodied spirits playing baseball in heaven. When dreams come true we may say "I had faith," but it is really in times of difficulty and stress that faith flourishes, because faith "does not see"! *O take my hand, dear Father, and lead Thou me.*

(--from Hymn 292, Service Book and Hymnal; Julia Hausmann.)

DETACHMENT

. . . they were strangers and foreigners on earth (Hebrews 11:8-16; v. 13).

To desire "a better country" is not to deny the goodness of the material world created by the Word of God. The better country, the heavenly one, is God's kingdom, God's rule, the new creation. The challenge for Christians is to learn detachment from earthly government in order to desire the kingdom that is the Father's good pleasure to give us. *Thy kingdom come, heavenly Father.*

FOR THE WARRIORS

A king is not saved by his great army (Psalm 33:12-22; v. 16).

We fall in love with "strong" leaders, and those who would be leaders outdo each other in flaunting their macho feathers. The art of warfare is pretty much summed up in strike and retaliation, strike and retaliation. The result is dead and wounded, dead and wounded. "The war horse is a vain hope for victory" (v. 17), but "our soul waits for the Lord" (v.20). For all of the warriors of the world, there is peace, reconciliation and forgiveness through Jesus Christ. *Make me an instrument of the peace of Christ, O God.*

THE FATHER'S PLEASURE

"Do not be afraid, little flock" (Luke 12:32-40; v. 32).

There are reasons to be afraid. One of the things we fear is weakness, powerlessness, fragility. The kingdom begins in a small, fragile way, like a mustard seed, but grows large (Matthew 13:31). When Paul complained about his mysterious thorn in the flesh, the Lord told him "power is made perfect in weakness" (2 Corinthians 12:9). The power of God to redeem the world from sin and death occurred in the weakness of the cross. Do not be afraid, weak, insignificant, little flock! The Father has pleasure in giving you his kingdom. *Emboldened by your Spirit, may I give my fears to you, Lord God, in Jesus' Name.*

YOUR TREASURE

"For where your treasure is, there your heart will be also (Luke 12:32-40; v. 34).

The heart follows the treasure, not the other way around. If your treasure is hidden away in some dark vault, that is where your heart will be. If your treasure is parked in the hot and dusty garage, that is where your heart will be. If our treasure is engaged in God's mission in the world, that is where our heart will be. For hearts to be warmed for the sake of the gospel of Jesus Christ, first the treasure needs to be baptized and consecrated to God through Jesus Christ. *Make me aware, heavenly Father, of where my heart really is.*

UPSIDE DOWN

. . . the master . . . will fasten his belt . . . and serve them (Luke 12:32-40; v. 37).

This little parable of Jesus is based on a preposterous premise. Everything is turned around—a master who serves his slaves! Wonderment and a wide smile across our face is the reaction. The gospel turns things upside down. Sinners are forgiven; God serves us. "The one who knew no sin became sin so that in him we might become the righteousness of God" (2 Corinthians 5:21). By showering such honor and glory on us it is God who is glorified and exalted. *Praise, glory, honor and thanksgiving to you, O God, for all your gifts, through Christ our Lord.*

THE HAMMER OF GOD: PART I

Is not my word like fire . . . and like a hammer that breaks a rock in pieces? (Jeremiah 23:23-29; v. 29).

The stubborn heart that seeks its own will, pleasure and purpose is the rock that is broken to pieces by God's Word. The cross of Christ shows us how serious the problem of sin is. God is no less serious about breaking down our resistance to righteousness, so that we can be restored to God's presence through Christ. This, after all, is God's final purpose. *I pray for a heart of flesh instead of a lifeless stone.* *

---

* "Heart of flesh for lifeless stone" from the hymn *God, my Lord, my Strength,* No. 484 in *Lutheran Book of Worship,* translated by Jaroslav J. Vajda.

THE HAMMER OF GOD: PART II

Is not my word like fire . . . and like a hammer that breaks a rock in pieces? (Jeremiah 23:23-29; v. 29).

God's word burns away all nonsense from our speech and thought, smashing whatever foolish ideas and plans we have devised. When the prophets are finished with us, God's word comes to us in Jesus Christ to mend, restore, forgive, and sculpt us into the New Creation. *Crush me and heal me, O God, in Jesus' Name.*

LANDMARKS

". . . why do you not know how to interpret the present time? (Luke 12:49-56; v. 56).

It is hard to make sense of the rapid changes in technology and popular culture. For many it is even harder to come to terms with shifting religious, spiritual and moral expectations. Perhaps we are intimidated by the demands for change, yielding convictions for the sake of accommodation, or perhaps we have simply lost our bearings. The landmarks, as always, are God's word as Law and Gospel. Sin is real, and so is grace. *Lord, keep us steadfast in your word.* (from Luther's hymn, *Lutheran Book of Worship,* 230)

GOD'S JUDGMENT

Give justice to the weak and the orphan (Psalm 82; v. 3).

The "gods" of this world come under the judgment of the God revealed to us in Jesus Christ. Whatever economic or governmental system that does not protect the weak, the orphan, the lowly and the destitute stands condemned. The "gods" we have fashioned to please ourselves are mortal; none will last very long. Our hope is that God will "rise up" to "judge the earth," because "all the nations belong to you." *Protect us, dear God, from indifference to the plight of the unprotected.*

A CLOSE VOTE

. . . division . . . three against two and two against three . . . (Luke 12:49-56; vv. 51, 52).

When they call for a "division of the house" you know the vote will be close. Winners will be happy and losers might be sore. When the church is divided, we just hope we are on the right side. We should not be too quick to claim that Jesus is on our side. Rather, we confess that, whether we are right or wrong, we trust that it is the righteousness of Jesus, and not our own, that will avail for us. *On the right side or the wrong side, help us to love each other, for Jesus' sake.*

SOMETHING BETTER

. . . stoned . . . sawn in two . . . persecuted . . . wandered in deserts . . . (Hebrews 11:29-12:2; vv. 37, 38).

Here is a promotional brochure for engaging new Christians that no one can refuse! Who wouldn't sign up to be sawn in two? When God enters human history in Jesus Christ to put down sin, death and evil there is a reaction, and the cross of Jesus is the largest sign of the "Division!" that Jesus arouses. Nevertheless, for the sake of "something better" our ancestors in the faith endured everything in order to "know Jesus, the power of his resurrection and the fellowship of his sufferings" (Philippians 3:10). *For the sake of the joy set before us, grant us faith that endures.*

FORMER ATTRACTIONS

. . . looking to Jesus the pioneer and perfecter of our faith (Hebrews 11:29-12:2; v. 2).

To fix our eyes on Jesus it is first necessary to turn away from something else. The attractions that formerly held us captive—making money or a name, pursuing pleasure or entertainment, or merely lost in self-absorption—now go on without us. Jesus perfects our faith by leading us on the path of service to neighbor and devotion to God. It is the way of the cross, endured for "the sake of the joy" that is set before us. *In the joy of the resurrection let the former things have no power over me.*

ON THE SABBATH

"Woman, you are set free . . . on the Sabbath day" (Luke 13:10-17; v. 12).

The heart of the story, of course, is that the woman was finally free of suffering after many years. Glory be to God! Those who are afraid of God's power will always find a way to object. The objection, however, points us to our own redemption. The Sabbath rest reminds us that while we were doing nothing, God, by the power of Christ's death and resurrection, freed us from whatever binds us. *By your word, Lord Jesus, I am free!*

AN UPRIGHT POSITION

Immediately she stood up straight (Luke 13:10-17; v. 13).

The hand of Jesus lifts the burden, loosens the shackles, and liberates the spirit from whatever oppresses us. Standing up straight is also part of the cure. If we are used to being bent over, or bound by an old attitude or behavior, we might need some encouragement to see how life looks from an upright position. Jesus Christ frees you! Discover the difference! *Lord, help me to see things clearly from this new perspective.*

> *"There comes a moment when people who have been dabbling in religion . . . suddenly draw back. Supposing we really found Him? We never meant it to come to that! Worse still, supposing He had found us?"* --C.S. Lewis (1898-1963)

BLESS THE LORD: PART I

Do not forget all his benefits (Psalm 103: v. 2).

Forgiveness, healing, lifting up from despair, and love and mercy poured out as the crowning touch—these are things to remember! Sometimes it is hard to believe in forgiveness. Things we have done or said haunt us and won't leave our restless thoughts alone. What is to be remembered above all is God's forgiveness through Jesus Christ. When brought low by remembrance of past sins, let God raise you up from the Pit by not forgetting that God "forgives all your iniquity." *When the unpleasant memories assail me, remind me that I am forgiven, for Jesus Christ's sake.*

BLESS THE LORD: PART II

. . . who heals all your diseases . . . (Psalm 103: v. 3).

The news comes: tests for one, cancer for another, an accident for someone else. Prayers are said, and some recover and some succumb. In the mystery of faith, we have learned to distinguish between "healing" and "a cure." People can be healed even if their illness is not cured. The grace and power of God in Jesus Christ brings a healing that goes beyond symptoms and vital signs. Even if illness reveals our mortality, God's final word is resurrection and life through Jesus Christ. *Be merciful, O God, to those who are suffering on this day; in Jesus' Name.*

BLESS THE LORD: PART III

. . . who redeems your life from the Pit (Psalm 103; v. 4).

Long before we knew anything about "the pits" the psalmist was already glorying in the fact that God lifts us up from the depths, from "the pits." The good news is not that the pits (sin, disease, tragedy, death) do not exist. The good news is that in the cross of Jesus, God comes to us there, in the pts, and redeems us. *I welcome your Presence, Lord God, wherever I happen to be.*

OPPRESSION

If you remove the yoke . . . you shall be like a watered garden . . . (Isaiah 58:9-14; vv. 9 11).
Oppression works both ways. Oppressed and oppressor both suffer. When we exploit or mistreat or ignore the pleas of "the hungry and the afflicted," we also feel the weight of their affliction. When we put away the accusing finger and speak well of our neighbor, we also experience the liberation of forgiveness. Our neighbor's well-being is also our well-being. *Help me to cultivate a forgiving spirit, heavenly Father.*

DOING NOTHING

. . . if you call the Sabbath a delight . . . (Isaiah 58:9-14; v. 13).
Businesses and services are proud to announce they are 24/7. They never close and they never rest. How sad. God's Sabbath promise is that, even if we put away our tools one day out of seven, *in order to do nothing,* God will provide daily bread anyway! On the Sabbath, we make our way to Divine Service, where we do nothing and *God does everything:* serving us by bringing grace, mercy and peace in word and sacrament through Jesus Christ. The Sabbath is no longer a duty but a delight. *Thanks and praise to you, heavenly Father, for the Day of Rest.*

SECRET JOY

"And you will be blessed because they cannot repay you" (Luke 14:7-14; v. 14).
The danger of inviting friends and rich neighbors to dinner is that—God forbid!—they will invite you in turn to their house. The blessing is found when our hospitality cannot be repaid. We can

never repay God's love for us. We become signs of that love when we are gracious to those who cannot possibly pay us back. Being instruments of God's love is our secret source of joy. *Heavenly Father, I pray for the gift of graciousness.*

EXALTATION AND HUMILITY

"All who exalt themselves will be humbled, and those who humble themselves will be exalted" (Luke 14:7-14; v. 11).

Jesus takes a common sense proverb and transforms it into a spiritual value. There is virtue in humility, especially before God. If we put ourselves forward as examples of goodness, there is not much Christ can do for us. If we come as sinners asking for mercy, God will raise us up and clothe us with the virtue of Christ. *Lord Jesus Christ, Son of God, have mercy upon me, a sinner.* *

---

*This is the ancient "Jesus Prayer". It apparently originated in Eastern Christianity and migrated westward. It is a 'breath prayer,' meant to be repeated over and over throughout the day, sometimes consciously, sometimes without even thinking about it.

LIGHT-BRINGERS

They rise up in the darkness as a light for the upright (Psalm 112; v. 4).

The upright also need the light, and very often the light comes from those who "fear the Lord." When a heavy cloud obscures and sun and we do not know which way to turn, the presence of a fellow believer, maybe even their words, will enlighten us and help us along. Our witness to each other and to those outside of the gospel will always be uneven, but if we trust God more than our self-confident ideas about God, we will illumine the path for those around us. *Help me to find the joy of Jesus in being a light-bringer.*

NEVER FORSAKEN

"I will never leave you or forsake you" (Hebrews 13:1-8; v. 5).

These comforting words were first spoken by Moses (Deuteronomy 31:6) and Joshua (Joshua 1:5) as the people of God were poised at the edge of the Promised Land. So we, always on the verge of discovering the newness of life that God has in mind for us, take courage from this promise. The writer of Hebrews points us to one aspect of that new life—being freed from the love of money and being content with what we have. This is daunting to the old nature, but in Christ we are transformed. It is this promise—I will not forsake you—that enables us to love God instead of money. *My Lord and my God, may I never leave you.*

HOSPITALITY: PART I

Do not neglect to show hospitality to strangers (Hebrews 13:1-8; v. 2).

Even when the 'welcome mat' is out, ordinarily we would not even think of allowing strangers into our homes. As citizens of "the city with foundations" perhaps we could at least consider the possibilities. Of course, we do not need to think only of our homes. Hospitality happens wherever we extend it. If we believe God is at work in our lives and in the world, who knows what divine messengers we will run into in the store, at work, in a classroom, or a chance encounter, maybe even in church? *Open my heart to thoughts of hospitality.*

HOSPITALITY: PART II

Do not neglect to show hospitality to strangers (Hebrews 13:1-8; v. 2).

We tend to find ways to extenuate biblical injunctions that seem too hard for us, or at least not practical. It is just exactly in the hard and impractical things that Christian discipleship most often reveals itself. We never know who will show up. Kings, angels, the Lord Christ Himself might appear at the door of our tent or tabernacle. The writer of Hebrews was probably thinking of Christian travelers who needed lodging and food and a good foot washing. Whether or not this or that stranger is a Christian, or no Christian, or Christ disguised, we'll just have to find out. *Surprise me, Lord Christ, in the people I meet.*

When a person loves his friend, it is by no means clear that he loves God. But when a person loves his enemy, it is clear that he fears and loves God, and only in this way can God be loved. —Søren Kierkegaard, 1813-1855

PRAYING FOR EACH OTHER

When I remember you in my prayers I always thank God (Philemon 4).

This is a wonderful introduction to intercessory prayer. Hold up your friend (or your enemy) in your mind's eye, and give thanks to God for the gifts, talents, and the faith of that person. It will help us to see what God is up to in our midst, and it will help us to love each other as God loves each one of us. Members of the body are mutually needy. In the Body of Christ, we need each other, because God has given gifts to each one for the well-being of the church. *Release me from all bitterness and jealousy, Lord to enable me to pray for my enemy, and really mean it.*

LIMITLESS LOVE

. . . when you perceive all the good we may do for Christ (Philemon 6).

The Letter to Philemon shows us the difference between obedience under compulsion and the freedom of the gospel. The Law is always limiting: Do this; Don't do that; whereas the gospel gives us the freedom to explore the limitless range of love for God and neighbor. We are slow to grasp some ideas—that a slave could be "a beloved brother", e.g.,--but God is patient with us. *Patient and forbearing God, enlighten the dullness of my thinking.*

DEEPLY ROOTED
. . . like trees planted by streams of water (Psalm 1; v. 3).
It's no mystery why trees betray the presence of a stream or river. It's also no mystery why loving, serving, forgiving, joyous Christians will be found near the Word of God, sinking roots deeper and deeper into Scripture, so that the life of Christ is drawn up into veins and arteries and becomes embodied in the believer. When everyone and everything else dries up, the one grounded in Scripture still bears fruit. *Like a tomato vine that never gives up, may I be a fruitful Christian into old age.*

LOVING JESUS
". . . even life itself . . ." (Luke 14:25-33; v. 26).
To love Jesus more than father and mother, spouse and children seems tame in comparison with the requirement of letting go even of "life itself." What we cling to most dearly is our life—the need for self-realization, time for me, the claim that I deserve this or that. Life under the gospel of Jesus Christ does not make sense to the unregenerated soul. Those renewed by the grace of the Lord Jesus understand perfectly the truth of Jesus' words, "Those who lose their life for my sake will find it" (Matthew 10:39).

HOLY CROSS DAY
SEPTEMBER 14
"Whoever does not carry the cross and follow me cannot be my disciple" (Luke 14:25-33).
September 14 is Holy Cross Day, but for Christians every day is the Day of the Holy Cross. Just as the Son of God entered into our suffering in order to bring us into a right relationship with God, so too, disciples of Jesus—those baptized into the crucified and risen

body of Christ—will find fellowship with Christ in solidarity with the suffering of the world. Caring for aged parents or a special needs child; or helping an addict whom everyone else has rejected; or risking your good name in supporting an unpopular cause; or merely giving up the "I'm too tired" or "Not my job" excuses—here we will find Christ and his disciples. *Lord, I praise you for those who really do carry the cross.*

"I'm giving up sarcasm for Lent; and it's really hard."
                                                    –An eight-year old girl

---

COUNTING THE COST
"For which of you, intending to build a tower, does not first sit down and estimate the cost?" (Luke 14:25-33; v. 28).
What will be have to give up to serve Christ today—anger, resentment, schemes design to hurt someone, thoughts we would be ashamed to reveal, a desperate clinging to money or possessions? When we enter the life "in Christ" we discover "the cost of discipleship," and at the same time we see how freeing it is to give up every burden. *Dear Jesus, it looks like self-denial is just as hard as taking up the cross.*

POSSESSIONS
". . . the cross . . . none of you can become my disciple if you do not give up all your possessions" Luke 1425-33; v. 33).
A garage sale with proceeds donated to charity is good for the soul, and a great aid to discipleship. Naturally we recoil at these words and wonder if Jesus is serious. Giving up "all our possessions" might feel like a cross, but it could be the other way around—the weight of possessions might just be the cross we are carrying around and did not know it. Traveling light makes the servant of Jesus more agile and sprightly. *Lighten my load, dear Jesus, even as I take your yoke upon me.*

112

THE ONLY GOD

'These are your gods, O Israel . . .' (Exodus 32:7-14; v. 8).
The irony is not lost on God. How soon God's own people forget who they are and how they got there. When the going gets tough in the wilderness we grasp at anything that is at hand that promises security and glory and make it our god. If there is nothing to grasp, we invent something. Security, prosperity, national defense, guns, maybe even a football team will serve as a god. Christ Jesus came into the world to save us from giving glory and honor to any except "to the King of the ages, the only God, immortal and invisible" (1 Timothy 1:17). *Sometimes it is tough, Lord. Remind me that you are with me, even in the wilderness.*

A PREFERENTIAL OPTION

. . . tax collectors and sinners . . . Pharisees and scribes . . . (Luke 15:1-10; vv. 1, 2).
One almost feels sorry for the righteous. Jesus seems to have a preferential option for the corrupt and the unregenerate. It is not that the 99 are abandoned. They are already righteous and have everything they need. Jesus' interest in sinners is to bring them back from their lost condition and restore them to a right relationship with God and with God's flock. Every single person on the face of the earth is precious, and no one can be missing. *Gracious God, I am only jealous of 'the one who is missing' when I forget that* I am *the one you have found.*

HE MINGLES

. . . the Pharisees and the scribes were grumbling . . . (Luke 15:1-10; v. 2).
Jesus does sometimes step over the line. He mingles not only with the respectable ones who follow the rules, but Jesus is also interested in those who, because of their lives or actions, have crossed the line into disrespectability. The power of God's grace is seen when lives

distorted by sin are straightened out once again. When the respectable ones start grumbling it may mean Jesus is up to something really interesting. *Praise to you, O God, for lives brought back to respectability, in Jesus' Name.*

THE LOVE OF GOD

. . . a new and right spirit within me (Psalm 51:1-12; v. 10).

When we realize that the love of God is poured into our hearts through the Holy Spirit (Romans 5:5) there is a change of heart, a different spirit, "a right spirit." The love of God poured into our hearts enables us to see people differently. The love of God enables us to trust God rather than fear our perceived enemies. It allows us to be generous even as we consider our own marginal situation. The love of God poured into our hearts makes our spirit right before God. *My heart is filling even now with your love, Lord God.*

GOD'S PURPOSE

. . . sinners—of whom I am the foremost. But for that very reason, I received mercy . . . (1 Timothy 1:12-17; vv. 15, 16).

The grace of God is for everyone, of course, but especially for those who have strayed far off course. The power of sin is overwhelmingly destructive, both for individuals as well as for society. God's purpose is not to finish the destruction that sin began, but to bring us back from the brink. If, in our madness, we are trying to blow the world apart, God's hand holds everything together through the power of the cross of Jesus Christ. *I believe, dear Jesus, that your grace is for me, too.*

GOD'S PLEASURE

Rejoice with me! (Luke 15:1-10; vv. 6, 9).

This is the picture of God that we should draw on our hearts and minds. People often think of God as a stern judge, and sometimes that image is appropriate. God's pleasure, however, is not in judging or condemning, but in finding, seeking, saving, rescuing, restoring. Leaving the ninety-nine alone might have been risky, but the joy of Jesus was finding the ones who were lost. That is where we will find joy as well. *Lord, give me a heart to reach the lost.*

24/7

We will make the shekel great (Amos 8:4-7; v. 5).

The greatness of the shekel is reported to us daily, actually minute to minute, in the corner of the television screen. 'Earnings' of the big companies are reported as 'news.' We stand in awe of rich people. Even if we are not wealthy, there aren't many of us who cannot say how much money we have in the bank or in our pocket. Day to day, hour by hour, our thoughts are more likely to center on 'the Almighty Dollar' rather than The Almighty God, creator of heaven and earth. Jesus frees us from captivity to the shekel, and enables us to receive from the Creator, by grace, all that money can offer, and even more! *Day by day, hour by hour, let your Spirit turn my loving, trusting thoughts to*
you, heavenly Father.

"When money is an idol, to be poor is a sin"
--William Stringfellow (1928-1985)

GOOD GOVERNMENT

I urge that . . . prayers . . . be made for everyone, for kings . . . (Timothy 2:1-7; vv. 1, 2).

"A quiet and peaceable life" is something we desire for all people, and it is connected with the commandment to love our neighbor as ourselves. To this end we pray for the well-being of our world and society, asking God to give to 'the king' and all in authority over us the wisdom to govern for the common good. We thank God for laws that order society and keep chaos at bay. We owe obedience to the laws of the land in which we live, but our allegiance is to Jesus

Christ alone as Lord. *Lord God, heavenly Father, Ruler of the nations, bless our President and all authorities, that they may govern with wisdom, promoting our common welfare and peace between nations; in Jesus' Name.*

SAINT MATTHEW, APOSTLE AND EVANGELIST
SEPTEMBER 21

"Follow me" (Matthew 9:9-13; v. 9).
We admire Matthew and the other disciples for their eagerness to follow Jesus. But if our only reaction is admiration, we miss the point. Jesus also calls us to follow him, to take his words seriously, to take up the cross through self-denial so that the life of Christ Jesus germinates and grows in us as well. Unless we are those who have "no need of a physician," Jesus came to draw us also into the power of his life and his righteousness. *In the footsteps of Matthew and the rest, I do wish to follow you, Lord Jesus Christ.*

THE POOR IN SIGHT
The LORD our God . . . seated on high . . . raises the poor from the dust . . . (Psalm 113; vv. 5, 7).
If the poor and needy are out of our sight, covered and hidden by the dust of their predicament, they are not hidden or ignored by God. Our inclination is to exalt ourselves by accumulating wealth or status. We may elevate ourselves so high that the poor and needy are lost from sight. God's throne is above earth and even above heaven, and yet God has the poor and needy in sight. If God is looking on the poor and needy, that is where we can look as well. *Heavenly Father, when I am face to face with the poor and needy, not only compassion, but I ask for wisdom as well.*

THE MANAGER
"There was a rich man who had a manager . . ." (Luke 16:1-2; v. 1).
The old word was steward, as in stewardship: caring for something that is not one's own. Great assets were entrusted to the manager in

our parable, with commensurate responsibilities. We do not know the nature of his squandering but it resulted in the end of his management. There is also for us an end, and an accounting. Wealth, talents, time, energy—all assets that are ours temporarily, to be managed to benefit the gospel of our Lord Jesus Christ. *Dear God, make me mindful of your assets under my stewardship.*

TOO MUCH LEFT OVER

". . . make friends . . . by means of dishonest wealth . . . " (Luke 16:1-13; v. 9).

Jesus is not shocked by debt reduction. Nor is Jesus appalled by the Robin Hood mentality of the dishonest manager. Wealth will be gone, one way or another. Either we will give it away or it will be taken from us at the gate of the eternal habitations. The parable suggests it might be embarrassing for us to show up with too much left over. *Dear God, I have money in my pocket. I do not know if I have "earned" it or merely "gotten" it. Help me to be wise in its use, for Jesus' sake.*

ONE MASTER

"No slave can serve two masters . . . You cannot serve God and wealth" (Luke 16:1-13; v. 13).

If you are a slave of the 'almighty dollar' you cannot be a servant of the Lord Jesus Christ. It is that simple. No one can serve two masters. There are many long outstretched arms clutching at us for allegiance, but only Jesus Christ can be our Master. Many things are important, but only the Lord Jesus Christ is of ultimate concern. *O God, grant that I may be a single-minded follower of the Lord Jesus Christ.*

117

VI. Even So, Come, Lord Jesus

Once again our hearts are stirring,
Waiting for the feast recurring.
Christ will come, but seems unhurrying:
Even so, Lord Jesus, come!

When our lives become disjointed,
Trust the One whom God appointed,
Jesus Christ, the Lord's anointed:
Even so, Lord Jesus, come!

To the Lord we're now returning;
God's abounding grace not spurning;
For that steadfast love we're yearning:
Even so, Lord Jesus, come!

On their knees the exiles praying
For that Day so long delaying;
Spirit and the Church are saying:
Even so, Lord Jesus, come!

GOD'S WILL

Alas for those who are at ease in Zion . . . (Amos 6:1, 4-7; v. 1)

Our "ease" may be the result of honest work, free of exploitation. Nevertheless, God does not want us to fail to recognize the suffering of our neighbor. It is God's will and purpose that everyone should live in peace and enjoy the fruit of vine and fig tree. It is also God's will that those who are "at ease in Zion" should have compassion wherever there is suffering. *Forgive my lack of compassion.*

AT THE GATE

". . . at his gate lay a poor man . . ." (Luke 16:19-31; v. 20).

Houses used to be built with wide porches facing the street so that the home was also hospitably open to the fellowship of passersby. Modern homes seems to be built with their backs to the street and located in "gated" communities. In this parable about the use of wealth, Jesus tells us that, if we will just lift up our eyes, we will nearly always see a need of some kind right at our gate. *Dear Jesus, help me to be a compassionate neighbor.*

THE ONE WHOM GOD HELPS

"The poor man died" (Luke 16:19-31; v. 22).

This is a classic case of the sin of omission—simply not doing something one ought to do. The sad, miserable life of the well-named Lazarus (*one whom God helps)* comes to an end, but the real tragedy here is that the unnamed rich man no longer has any chance of doing anything for the poor man. It was not Lazarus but the rich man who ran out of time! Opportunities to be rich in good works are all around us. Let all be done in Jesus' Name. *Dear God, let me be the help Lazarus is looking for, before it is too late.*

The Great Reversal

"Child, remember that during our lifetime you received your good thigs, and Lazarus in like manner evil things; but now he is comforted here, and you are in agony" (Luke 16:19-31; v. 25).

When all hope was lost, Sarah gave birth. When the people could suffer no more, the Lord sent Moses. When they were preparing burial spices, Jesus was raised from the dead. Child, remember: Neither despair of your situation nor be proud of it, because God is the God of reversals. *At all times I will trust you, O Lord, for my well-being.*

Election Day

Do not put your trust in princes, in mortals, in whom there is no help (Psalm 146: v. 3).

This psalm should be required reading for all leaders, civic or ecclesiastical, elected or not. All of us are fallible and stand under the judgment as well as the grace of God. We pray that God will endow our leaders with wisdom so that our nation follows paths that enhance the common good for all people of the world. Since righteousness eludes human effort so easily, we acknowledge that our help and our hope come from the Lord our God. *Heavenly Father, grant us leaders that reflect your goodness.*

Verses Frequently Misquoted

For the love of money is a root of all kinds of evil . . . (1 Timothy 6:6-10; v. 10).

In one of the FMQV (Frequently Misquoted Verses) of the Bible, the writer tells us that it is not money as such, but the *love* of it, from which all kinds of evil rise. Money, like time or talent, is a resource to be used for good or ill. When we caress it, hold it tightly, count it over and over, it will lead us to make poor choices. When we place money in God's hands for a godly purpose, we won't even miss it. *Help me to fear, love, and trust you, O God, above everything else.*

POURING OUT

In their eagerness to be rich some have wandered away from the faith and pierced themselves with many pains (1Timothy 6:6-19; v. 10).

Our society admires and encourages prosperity. Our Lord Jesus, however, calls us to a life of service to God and neighbor. Our life under Christ is characterized by pouring out rather than gathering in. Stress and anxiety are sometimes the result of pursuing the wrong dream. Obedience to Christ and trust in God are the best ways to deal with emotions that upset us *Save me, dear God, from the self-inflicted wounds of unhealthy desires.*

NEITHER THANKS NOR PRAISE

"Increase our faith . . . We are worthless slaves; we have done only what we ought to have done" (Luke 17:5-10; vv. 5, 10).

Jesus taught forgiveness (vv. 1-4), and the disciples said, "Increase our faith." To forgive and to serve both spring from our faith in Christ. We forgive because we are forgiven, and we serve because Christ served us. To serve expecting neither thanks nor praise will happen only on the basis of faith. *Holy Spirit, increase my faith.*

GOD'S TIMETABLE

. . . a vision . . . wait for it . . . (Habakkuk 2:1-4; v. 3).

The prophet with the strange name has the same complaint that we have. God sees violence and wickedness in the world but doesn't seem to do anything about it. God's timetable is not ours. The vision God has given us is the final victory over sin, death and evil through Jesus Christ. This is our hope and confidence that we write in bold letters and in large font. While others reach for desperate measures, Christian folk will be faithful and steadfast in their trust that all will be well, because Christ is Lord. *When you do not act, Lord, it makes it harder for us to explain your goodness. Nevertheless, increase my faith.*

WAITING

How long shall I cry for help . . . I will keep watch to see what he will say to me (Habakkuk 2:1-4; v. 1).

The hardest part is always the waiting. Whether for a lab report, or for a job, or waiting for the phone to ring, or waiting for God's help—it is the waiting that brings us down. Waiting is an essential part of faith, even a huge part. In spite of setbacks, discouragement, meager results, prolonged agony, and waiting, waiting for the Lord, we believe the Lord's answer will come through the cross and for Jesus Christ's sake. *Lord God, while I am waiting silently, increase my faith.*

FRET NOT

Commit your way to the Lord; trust in him, and he will act (Psalm 37:1-9; v. 5).

Trying to influence or control the actions and behavior of other people is a cause of anxiety or, as the psalmist puts it, fretting. When we follow Jesus, we can expect that much of our lives will be lived out in the shadow of the cross. Though there are glimpses along the way, resurrection is always a promise that can only be grasped by faith. Behind the turmoil there is a final, glorious conclusion in Jesus Christ. We commit "out way," our lives, to this promise and to this God. *I am trusting you, Lord Jesus; / Never let me fall. / I am trusting you forever / And for all.* (Havergal, *Lutheran Book of Worship*, #460).

THE APOSTLES' TEACHING

Hold to the standard of sound teaching (2 Timothy 1:8-14; v. 13).

It seems the possibility of following unreliable teachers was present from the very beginning. In our day anyone with the first month's rent can start a "church" and anoint oneself bishop. Against this, the pattern of life depicted in the Book of Acts will keep us centered: "They devoted themselves to the apostles' teaching and fellowship, to the breaking of bread and the prayers" (Acts 2:42). *Center me always, Holy Spirit, in Jesus Christ.*

OUR WITNESS

Do not be ashamed . . . of the testimony about our Lord (2 Timothy 1:1-14; v. 8).

If we did not run the risk of being ashamed of the gospel, the apostle would not have to urge us *not* to be ashamed. In a world enthralled by power, prosperity, and success, we bear witness to God who, in Jesus Christ, died in weakness, humility, and shame on a cross. It is just exactly in weakness that God's power over sin, death and evil is revealed. If we are reticent, the Spirit will embolden our witness. *Holy Spirit, make me bold, for Jesus' sake.*

EVEN THIS MUCH

"Increase our faith!" . . . 'we have done only what we ought to have done" (Luke 17:5-10; vv. 5, 10).

It would be nice, and it would surely inflate or egos, if someone applauded and slapped us on the back every time we did something "Christian." Our need for recognition only reveals the shallowness of our faith. Our faith, according to the measurement Jesus proposes, is something less than the size of a mustard seed. If we don't have enough faith to uproot a tree, we can at least believe that in Jesus Christ we are freed from sin, including the sin of self-centeredness. Even this much faith frees us to serve in Jesus' name, which in itself is its own reward. *Increase my service, in Jesus' Name.*

A GOOD WASHING

"Wash and be clean" (2 Kings 5:7-15; vv. 10, 13).

Our relationship with God does not need to be complicated. Others may have taken a long and convoluted path until they found God's grace, but that does not need to be our story. We have already been washed in baptism. Let us not disdain that small splash, for in it the word of God's promise in Jesus Christ becomes true for us. Reclaim the gift of baptism for your healing and salvation, and for a genuinely good feeling! *You have washed me, O God. Help me to believe that I really am clean, for Jesus' sake.*

A REASONABLE RETURN: PART I

Ten lepers approached . . . one of them, when he saw he was healed, turned back, praising God with a loud voice (Luke 17:11-19; v. 15).

Ten percent is a reasonable rate of return on one's investment. If we are grateful ten percent of the time for ten percent of God's blessings, we can consider ourselves well on the way to spiritual maturity. It is often the case that those who have been far away from God are the most excited upon discovering grace. Grace is no less exciting for those who have experienced it continually over a long period of time. *Help me to see, once again, the wonder of your grace.*

A REASONABLE RETURN: PART II

One of them . . . turned back, praising God (Luke 17:11-19; v. 15).

Unless we are completely oblivious to what is happening, there are times when we shudder in utter amazement at what God is doing in our lives. In the midst of hardship and difficulty, stress and the oppression of guilt, God forgives, lifts up, protects and provides what we need for body and soul. The Samaritan who was healed began to count his blessings. He got as far as number one and began praising and glorifying God. *Lord, when I am stressed, teach me to count my blessings.*

A REASONABLE RETURN: PART III

". . . except this foreigner?" (Luke 17:11-19; v. 18).

Animosity towards outsiders was not invented by our generation. Jesus lived and worked among people suspicious and hateful of people who were considered different. In the group of ten whom Jesus healed at least one was a foreigner. All were blessed by God's gracious power. One was different, not because he was a foreigner, but because he realized that God had done something wonderful in his life. It is often the outsiders who make us aware of the greatness of the Lord. *Thank you, Lord Jesus, for healing us all.*

REDISCOVERING DELIGHT

Great are the works of the LORD, studied by all who delight in them. (Psalm 111; v. 2).

Some have wonderful stories to tell of deliverance from sin or danger. Many of us seem to have lived mundane and uninteresting lives by comparison. Even an uneventful life is something wonderful to be acknowledged and to give thanks for. One way to rub the dull patina from our faith is to recall, in a meditative way, the mighty acts of God in our lives. We may discover long lost delight. *When I remember all you have done for me, Lord God, I am amazed.*

THE OBVIOUS

Remember Jesus Christ . . . (2 Timothy 2:8-15; v. 8).

"Always remind people of the most obvious—it is what they most forget," said the sage. How could we forget Jesus? But it is so easy to do, not only in the days full of obligations and activities, but even at church where there are friends to talk with, news to catch up on, things to sign up for. Remember Jesus Christ: who in his death and resurrection frees us and the world from sin, death and the power of evil. *Jesus. I remember.*

FAITHFULNESS
. . . if we are faithless, he remains faithful (2 Timothy 2:8-15; v. 13).
Our passion for God grows hot and cold. Our desire to be under the yoke of discipleship varies from day to day according to the direction of the wind. We boast of faith but cannot fool ourselves about the reality of our doubts. We are saved by faith, which is good news. However, the even better news is that we are saved by the faithfulness of God. When faith fades, the fuse that reignites our faith is the word that God remains faithful to us, regardless of how the winds are blowing today. *I thank you, heavenly Father, that your faithfulness never wanes.*

COMING AND GOING: PART I
From where will my help come? (Psalm 121; v. 1).
When things get tense it is not hard to find where the idols are. What we hang on to most dearly is probably the source of our "help." In the day of trouble some look to finances or 'things' to see them through; others turn to the fortress of 'security' or 'way of life.' God's Spirit gently turns our devotion from the things we regard as powerful to the God who not only created the mountains but also who shows his power over sin, death and evil in the death and resurrection of Jesus. *On the top of the hill or in the deepest valley, I know you are with me.*

COMING AND GOING: PART II
. . . neither slumber nor sleep (Psalm 121; v. 4).
Our well-being depends on the turning of the earth on its axis. We welcome daylight as it comes our way, and then we welcome the night, because we get tired. To be human is to need the rhythms of light and darkness, waking and sleeping. To be God is to be awake, alert, ever watchful over us, protecting us from fears at night and dangers in the day. Jesus Christ is the sign of God's Presence among

us. *In peace I lie down and in joy I awake, because you are always watching.*

COMING AND GOING: PART III

The LORD will keep you from all evil (Psalm 121; v. 7).

Our emotions are easily aroused by thoughts and warnings of danger and terror. In times like these we will discover straightway where we have placed our trust. While surrounded by fear, we Christians have an opportunity to make a bold, counter-intuitive witness: *Our help comes from the Lord!* Especially when uncertainty grasps us, we believe that God is faithful. Jesus taught us to pray, *Deliver us from evil.*

COMING AND GOING: PART IV

The LORD will keep your going out and your coming in from this time on and forevermore (Psalm 121; v. 8).

Even if you never venture far from your front door, life never stays the same. We are going and coming, growing and learning, welcoming and saying good-bye, acquiring new skills and leaving behind the things we used to do. The changes in our lives can be abrupt and disconcerting. Through it all, the Lord watches over us and grants us protection. *Lord God, whether I am coming and going, keep me centered on serving you.*

SAINT LUKE, EVANGELIST
OCTOBER 18

Jesus told them a parable about their need to pray always and not to lose heart (Luke 18:1-8; v. 1).

One of the things Luke the Evangelist bears witness to is prayer. Prayer is not easy. "Some days the hardest thing I have to do is to pray," said one bishop. In prayer there are some needs we can feel and easily identify. There are other needs we vaguely sense but have a hard time discovering their nature. Jesus tells us we have a need to pray . . . always . . . without losing heart. Many people avoid prayer.

128

Avoiding prayer is just as harmful as avoiding water. We need to pray, and when we do, we find the same kind of satisfaction that a drink of cool water brings. *Holy Spirit, teach me to pray.*

THE STRUGGLE OF PRAYER

. . . limping . . . (Genesis 32:22-31; v. 31).

What stamina! What strength! The wrestling match lasted all night until the first rays of dawn. Neither Jacob nor his mysterious opponent could gain the upper hand. Jacob sensed the Divine Presence and asked for a blessing. What he got was a limp, and a new name. When we encounter God, whether in word or sacrament or prayer, we will be changed. "In Christ, there is a new creation" (2 Corinthians 5:17). *O God, you meet me in prayer, and you will change me. Help me not to be afraid.*

THE WORD OF GOD

. . . you have known the sacred writings (2 Timothy 3:14-17; v. 15).

They read Bible stories to us and they "placed in our hands the Holy Scriptures." We paid attention to the public reading of Scripture on the Lord's Day. Perhaps we even memorized shorter or longer portions of Scripture. (And if not, it is never too late to begin!). The point of all this attention to Scripture is to "instruct us for salvation through faith in Jesus Christ." We immerse ourselves in Scripture because this is where we learn the Way, the Truth and the Life. *Holy Spirit, lead me to Christ through your holy word.*

A MIGHTY FORTRESS: PART I

God is our refuge and strength, a very present help in trouble (Psalm 46; v. 1).

We want stability, but we know that, in this life, changes are inevitable; the roaring of bombs and gunfire robs us of tranquility; and the constant cries for justice make the complacent tremble. The Lord God calms our anxiety by ordering us to "Be still." When our weapons fall silent we are once again able to regain our perspective, enabling us to put our trust in God, who alone is our refuge and very present help in trouble. *Therefore, we will not be afraid.*

A MIGHTY FORTRESS: PART II

Therefore we will not fear, though the earth should change (Psalm 46; v. 2).

"Life will never be the same" was the universal response to September 11. Now, more than ever, we have discovered what things are truly important, and we have discovered exactly where our trust is placed. Though heaven and earth fall apart, those who trust in the God revealed by our Lord Jesus Christ will not fear. *The Lord of hosts is with us; the God of Jacob is our refuge.*

A MIGHTY FORTRESS: PART III

. . . though the earth should change . . . (Psalm 46; v. 2).

We used to think that the earth could never change. Then the glaciers began to melt. "Heaven and earth will pass away" (Mark 13:31) Jesus tells us, though we may not believe it. Change takes place all over—in our homes and families, where we work. Even the church experiences change, now and then. What does not change is the promise that God is our refuge and strength, our *Mighty Fortress.* The sign and seal of the promise is Jesus Christ, our bulwark against all threats to our well-being. *The earth melts at the sound of your voice, O God, but our hearts are steadfast in Christ.*

A MIGHTY FORTRESS: PART IV

He breaks the bow and shatters the spear (Psalm 46; v. 9).

"The old Satanic foe / Has sworn to work us woe." Sin and guilt; war abroad and danger at home; hardship in providing for our daily needs—all signs of Satan's woe. In Christ God frees us from sin's power, and gives us courage to pursue peace with our perceived enemies. Whether we regard nations, religions, or neighbors to be our foe, when we lay down our weapons and animosity melts into friendship one can see how the abstract concept of justification reshapes our reality. *O God, I put my bow and spear into your hands, trusting in Christ the Victor.*

[God] must perform an alien work—which is to convict—until he comes to his proper work—which is to comfort and to proclaim grace. –"Formula of Concord: Solid Declaration, Article V: Law and Gospel." In *Book of Concord*, Robert Kolb and Timothy J. Wengert, eds. Minneapolis: Fortress Press. © 2000. p. 583

GOD'S PROPER WORK
. . . the righteousness of God has been disclosed . . . (Romans 3:19-28; v. 21).

We always knew God was "righteous" by definition. Some may think the righteousness of God is revealed in punishment of the wicked. That would be fine for our enemies, not so good for us. Now the curtain is drawn back. We hold our breath. God's righteousness is disclosed in . . . the forgiveness of sins! God shows that he is good and upright by forgiving our sins for Jesus Christ's sake. This is God's "proper work", as the Reformers put it. *It is just exactly today, now, that I need your righteousness, gracious God, in Jesus' Name.*

THE HOLY ONES: PART I
. . . the holy ones . . . shall receive the kingdom (Daniel 7:13-18; v. 18)

Much of our life is spent waiting for a breakthrough. Plans are laid out but forces larger than ourselves determine the outcome. "Time and chance" (Ecclesiastes 9:11) are not always on our side. God, however, is for us (Romans 8:31). In Jesus Christ God has broken through the barriers of sin and death. "Dominion, glory and kingship" (v. 14) have been given to Christ, and we are his. Whatever confines or oppresses only leads us to pray more fervently, *Your kingdom come.*

THE HOLY ONES: PART II

"Love your enemies" (Luke 6:20-31; v. 35)

This command of Jesus is guaranteed to make us grind our teeth. You don't have to have strong political ideas to have an enemy. It is enough to consider those who in one way or another make life difficult. Some say things that are not true. Another snubs us, for no apparent reason. There is that prickly personality with no self-awareness. Our impulse is to wring their necks. Instead, Jesus tells us to love them. "We love because he first loved us." *O God, melt the hardness of my heart.*

THE HOLY ONES: PART III

"Love your enemies" (Luke 6:20-31; v. 35).

If this command came out of the blue, with no warning, it would fall on deaf ears and unreceptive hearts. The key is, "To you that listen . . ." If our objective is to be disciples, followers, obedient to the call of Jesus Christ, the command to Love Your Enemies makes perfect sense. Jesus did not come to keep the world as it is, where enemies hate each other. Jesus came to forgive sinners and reconcile enemies. Love Your Enemy makes perfect sense to us who have been forgiven and reconciled to God through Jesus Christ. *Lord Jesus, you really turn things upside down. Let me share in this joy and wonderment.*

THE HOLY ONES: PART IV

The LORD takes pleasure in his people (Psalm 149; v. 4)

The cars line up to get on the freeway. Kids are looking for their shoes. Coffee is brewing. People check their e-mails. Life is sometimes good, sometimes bad, sometimes normal, sometimes tragic. Through it all, the Lord takes pleasure in his people whom he loves unconditionally in Jesus Christ. *I take pleasure in your love for me, Lord God.*

THE HOLY ONES: PART V
"Do unto others as you would have them do to you" (Luke 6:20-31; v. 31)
What's good for me is good for you. If I show a card to take care of medical expenses, I want you to have one, too. If I enjoy certain benefits, I want the same right for you. If I have food and am warm (or cool), I want the same for you. It all springs from what God has done for us in Jesus Christ. What God has—power over sin and death, perfect fellowship in the Trinitarian inner life—God shares with us through Jesus Christ. *Lord God, give me a heart ready to share all good things; in Jesus' Name.*

THE HOLY ONES: PART VI
I have heard . . . of your love toward all the saints (Ephesians 1:15-23; v. 15).
Christian faith is not just about the idea of love; faith becomes active, real, through real deeds and actions. It is important to think good thoughts about fellow believers; it is even more important to give concrete expression to the love we feel in our hearts for each other. If it is sometimes hard to love, let us remember that God's love for us was revealed in the cross of Jesus Christ. *Dear Jesus, help me to bear the cross of my neighbor's needs.*

CHRIST THE ASCENDED LORD
. . . far above all rule and authority and power and dominion (Ephesians 1:15-23; v. 21).
Christ has died; Christ is risen; and Christ is the Ascended Lord who rises and rises and soars above all rulers of cities, provinces and nations. In spite of the arrogance and divisiveness of party spirit, Christ rules. Nations plot their own courses as though they were in control of history, but Christ is Sovereign who mysteriously uses

human events to bring about his own divine purpose and will. *Blessed be the Name of Jesus forever and ever.*

APOSTASIES

. . . our apostasies indeed are many . . . (Jeremiah 14:7-10; v. 7).
If only the Christian life were, in fact, like Jacob's ladder, "Ev'ry rung goes higher, higher." Alas! We stumble and fall. By grace we are picked up and straightened out, and we begin again. It is possible, because you, Lord Jesus, "are in the midst of us, and we are called by your name." By faith the grace of the Lord Jesus enables us to feel more acutely both the depth of sin as well as the ecstasy of forgiveness. *I am coming home, Lord, once again.*

GOD'S PEACE

. . . that . . . the message might be fully proclaimed . . . (2 Timothy 4:16-18; v. 17).
It is strange that the gospel of Jesus Christ, the good news of forgiveness and reconciliation with God and with our fellow human beings, should encounter opposition. Even one's friends may turn out to be obstacles because of self-interest, or lack of dedication, or failure of nerve to take on the powers and principalities that resist God's peace. Nevertheless, in this present age, in a population obsessed with the specter of terror, there is nothing more important than the message of God's peace through Jesus Christ. *Let your peace rule in my heart, Lord Jesus.*

WE ARE HAPPY

My soul longs, indeed it faints for the courts of the LORD (Psalm 84; v. 2).
The late bishop Anthony Bloom told of a man in France who sat in an empty church, staring at the crucifix for hours on end. "What are you doing here?" they asked. "He looks at me, and I look at him, and we are happy," the man replied. Some people go to church out

of a sense of duty, and some go because they just want to be with God. These are the hearts that "sing for joy", even if they can't sing. *Heavenly Father, sometimes it is enough just to know I am in your Presence.*

THOSE PEOPLE

"God, I thank you that I am not like other people" (Luke 18:9-14; v. 11).

Of course, we really are like other people. Perhaps the only difference between us and the more notorious sinners is lack of opportunity. If the gospel is for redemption and transformation of the lives of thieves, rogues and adulterers, the gospel will certainly redeem sinners who fly just under the radar, too. Then there comes the sacrifice of thanksgiving, and all the glory belongs to God. *Lead us not into Temptation.*

THIS ONE

"God, be merciful to me, a sinner!" (Luke 18:9-14; v. 13).

Many Christians use the so-called "Jesus Prayer." *Lord Jesus Christ, Son of God, have mercy on me, a sinner.* This phrase is repeated over and over, without ceasing (1 Thessalonians 5:17), consciously and unconsciously, throughout the day and night. Sometimes it is abbreviated to "Jesus, have mercy," or even simply, "Jesus." The backdrop to this prayer is the promise, "This one went down to his home justified." "Kyrie eleison." *Lord, have mercy.*

KEEP THE FAITH

I have kept the faith (2 Timothy 4:6-8; v. 7).

God grant that all of us may faithfully confess Jesus Christ as Lord to our dying breath. Personal faithfulness is important, but there is more here than that. "The faith" is the essential proclamation about Jesus that comprises the gospel. Nothing is added, and nothing taken away. It is what parents teach their children, and pastor teach their flocks. "The faith" is what theologians defend against perversions of the gospel. Keeping the faith ultimately means passing it on. *Thank you, Lord, for all who have faithfully lived and died in Christ.*

"Tradition is the living faith of the dead. Traditionalism is the dead faith of the living."   –Jaroslav Pelikan (1923-2006)

The Resurrection Age
"Those who belong to this age . . ." (Luke 20:27-38; v. 34).
We live in the tension between "this age" and "that age." We embrace and enjoy the things of "this age" that God has created—family, food, laughter, sunsets, etc. But we do not "belong" to this age, characterized as it is by sin, death and evil and all their symptoms. We belong to "that age," the resurrection age, marked by life in unimaginable richness, made possible by the death and resurrection of Jesus. *Let me not be so tightly bound to the things of today that I miss the glory of your New Day.*

Sellers of Fear
. . . not to be quickly shaken in mind or alarmed . . . (2 Thessalonians 2:1-5; v. 2).
Nothing stirs us up more than speculation about relating current events to supposed "Bible prophecy." When the Day of the Lord arrives, we will not need television preachers or "breaking news" bulletins to tell us. In the meantime, let the sellers of fear deal with their own anxieties. The people of Jesus Christ will serenely trust that God will protect us from every evil. *Thy kingdom come.*

What Will Be
. . . when I awake, I shall . . . behold your likeness (Psalm 17; v. 15).
Each morning is a resurrection, full of wonder and awe, that God has granted us another day of grace. The sun rises, the daily routine falls into place, and everything is sheer gift. One day we will not

wake up in familiar surroundings. Neither Iowa, nor Kansas, but a glory beyond description. "What we will be has not yet been revealed . . ." We do know this: we will be like him" (1 John 3:2). *"We believe in the resurrection of the body and the life everlasting."*

NOT VOLUNTEERS

. . . he called you . . . that you may obtain the glory of our Lord Jesus Christ (2 Thessalonians 2:13-17; v. 14).

We were not volunteers. We were "called." When we "share the good news" we are not inviting people to join a club or to fill empty pews. We are "calling" them to experience the glory of our Lord Jesus Christ. "Through the proclamation of the good news," the Holy Spirit has called us out of our meanness, self-centeredness, despair and fear to be raised into the glory of Jesus Christ who has conquered everything inglorious by his death and resurrection. *Holy Trinity, at baptism you called my name. And I say, 'Here am I.'*

SOMETHING EVEN BETTER

. . . in the resurrection . . . [they] neither marry or are given in marriage (Luke 20:27-38; v. 35).

Jesus blesses human marriage, because the Father has blessed it. "God blessed them and said, 'Be fruitful and multiply" (Genesis 1:28). When a man and woman live together faithfully, the angels rejoice. As wonderful as human love in marriage is, there is something even better: the resurrection life fulfills all desires and all needs. Nothing could be added to improve it, not even marriage! *In your presence there is fullness of joy* (Psalm 16:11).

WOUNDED WORLD

. . . the sun of righteousness will rise with healing . . . (Malachi 4:1-2; v. 2).

Wickedness is its own enemy, and evil brings its own confusion and destruction. What we long for in God's judgment is not so much destruction as restoration. Jesus Christ, the Sun of Righteousness, comes to put the pieces of our own broken lives back together, and seals them in his grace. The arrogant always seem to have the upper hand, but as the day of Jesus Christ, the sun of righteousness, dawns, God's light brings healing to this deeply wounded world. *O God, I offer my brokenness to be mended by your grace.*

LAZY BELIEVERS

Keep away from believers who are living in idleness (2 Thessalonians 3:6-13; v. 6).

The thought of "the end of the world" drives people into frenzies of speculation and useless calculations. "Do not go after them," Jesus says. It is all idle chatter. God calls every Christian to a mission, or purpose. There is the long view of vocation stretching over years, and there is the immediate call for service or witness in the present moment. A task to serve our neighbor, a word to comfort the afflicted, a prayer—always something to keep God's faithful ones from idleness. *Holy Spirit, help me to be an energetic Christian.*

THE MEMORIAL FUND

. . . gifts dedicated to God . . . all will be thrown down (Luke 21:5-19; v. 5).

There are different ways of making sure we will not be forgotten. Brass plaques on a memorial gift to the church is one way. The temple in Jerusalem was also filled with memorial gifts. When the Romans came in 70 AD it all came crashing down. Our hope of glory is to be gathered into the grace of the Lord Jesus Christ and to follow him wherever the demands of discipleship take us. Whatever happens to impressive buildings or generous gifts, what endures is faith in Christ. *God, I am afraid of being forgotten. I know you never forget a name.*

JUDGMENT

. . . the LORD . . . is coming to judge the earth (Psalm 98: v. 9).

We are ambivalent about judgment. It's good for others, not so good for us. If we are gracious we will let God deal with the notoriously wicked. Our concern needs to be how we ourselves will fare. Judgment under the lordship of Jesus Christ is for cleansing, redemption, and salvation. Even though the mere mention of judgment gives us a chill, in our heart of hearts we want the cleansing and purifying grace of Jesus to free us from sin, death and evil. *Come, Lord Jesus!*

A DAY OF THANKSGIVING

"I am the bread of life" (John 6:25-35; v. 35).

On this day when gorging seems to be the national pastime and a full stomach our keenest desire, Jesus warns us about "the food that perishes." He offers himself as the high energy low calorie substitute. By faith in Christ the bread that gives life to the world satisfies our needs and leads us to share our bread with hungering bodies and hungering souls. *Father in heaven, give us this bread always.*

HARD TO TALK ABOUT JESUS

"I will give you words . . . " Luke 21:5-19; v. 15).

It is really hard to talk about our faith. It is really, really hard, to talk about Jesus, even with our own families and with people whom we know to be Christians. We should know that when we talk about Jesus it is not we who speak but the Holy Spirit using our lips and tongues. The words about Jesus are the words of Jesus himself. Whatever happens to the words and whether they bear fruit or not rests in the power of the Spirit. *Lord, I wonder why it is so hard to talk about my faith.*

KNOWING THE SIGNS

"Beware that you are not led astray" (Luke 21:5-19; v. 8).

There is a fascination with the end of all things, and crafty people exploit our willingness to think that anyone can actually know the future. The "sign" we should look for is to be aware of people who think they know the signs! "Do not go after them," Jesus says, because Jesus himself is our sign—the sign of God's forgiveness, life and salvation. *Help me to live faithfully today and trust you for tomorrow, heavenly Father.*

JESUS REMEMBERS

"Jesus, remember me . . ." (Luke 23:33-43; v. 42).

It is wonderful to remember old friends, even more wonderful to be remembered by them. We, who are needy and anxious, gather around the Lord Jesus, hoping for eye contact and a sign of recognition. We can be sure that Jesus remembers all for whom he died—how could he forget!—and the sign of his remembrance of us comes in the form of bread and wine: the body, the blood of Christ, *for you! Jesus, remember me when you come into your kingdom.*

GOD MADE VISIBLE

He is the image of the invisible God (Colossians 1:11-20; v. 15).

The God who spoke and it was so, who created the immeasurably vast heavens, now comes into focus in the One Individual, Jesus of Nazareth. The majesty and glory of God are revealed in this tiny spot of Light obscured for a time beneath human flesh, suffering and dying on a cross. Then in the light of the resurrection we see that it is in fact the cross that reveals God's glory, power and majesty to rescue us from the power of darkness. Jesus reveals God as the One Who Suffers for his people. *You are pleased, dear God, with your Son, our Savior, Jesus Christ.*

STILLNESS

Be still, and know that I am God (Psalm 46; v. 10).

The Twelve Step people have the right translation here: Let go and let God. The Lord wants to grasp the bow out of our hands and snap it in two; take our hands in his and relax our fists; put his hand over our mouth and calm our spirits. God is in charge, and there is nothing we can do about it. If there are battles to be fought, let God's Valiant Warrior deal with it all on the cross so that we and our enemies may be perfectly at peace with each other and with God. *I am done fighting, Lord God. The battle is yours, and the victory.*

A NEW WAY OF BEING

The soldiers also mocked him (Luke 23:33-43; v. 36). Jesus is a King who allows himself to be mocked by those who should be bending the knee before him. God's kingdom of justice through grace really is a new world superimposed on the old world we knew. A new way of being leaves all of us disoriented. God's justice is revealed in forgiveness. The king becomes a servant. Glory and honor come through cross and suffering. And we are excused if we struggle with the newness of it. *Give me a moment to think this through. Spirit of God; help me to believe it.*

CONVERSION

"Do you not fear God?" (Luke 23:33-43; v. 40).

We are often cynical about "jailhouse conversions." Claims of having "got religion" are easily dismissed as ploys to gain early parole. We do not always stop to consider the depth or reality of our own conversions. Are we followers of Jesus out of mere habit, or have we felt in our bones the terror of standing before God clothed only in our sinfulness? You who fear God, look to the cross of Jesus Christ for your acquittal! *I remember my most recent conversion, only a few moments ago.*

SAINT ANDREW'S DAY
NOVEMBER 30

"We have found the Messiah" (John 1:35-42; v. 41).

The Sunday closest to Saint Andrew's Day is the First Sunday in Advent. Saint Andrew thus leads the way into the new church year by announcing to his brother Peter, and to us, "We have found the Messiah." This in turn is the theme for everything we Christians do. To the skeptics, the indifferent, the self-sufficient and to the scoffers we say, "We have found the Messiah." Evangelism is not coercion, but proclamation and invitation. To all Jesus himself says, "Come and see." *Praise, glory and honor to you, O God, through Christ our Lord.*

www.ingramcontent.com/pod-product-compliance
Lightning Source LLC
LaVergne TN
LVHW092317080426
835509LV00034B/566